Contents

Tables

Department of Education and Science

9–13 Middle Schools

An illustrative survey

London
Her Majesty's Stationery Office

© Crown copyright 1983
First published 1983

ISBN 0 11 270556 1

Preface

This survey is concerned with 9–13 middle schools of which there were 610 in January 1983. The survey provides a detailed picture of 48 of these schools; this sample was chosen to illustrate a range of contexts.

Its main purposes were to assess how well these schools provided for the age range and how well the pupils responded to the education offered. As such it will be of particular interest to those local education authorities with 9–13 middle schools and to the heads and teachers who work in them.

But many of the findings will be of interest to all concerned with the 9–13 age range. They raise questions that apply to the top years of primary schools and to practices in the first two years of secondary schooling.

Some issues which were part of the background of the survey, such as the effect of falling rolls, the viability of small middle schools, and the match between the training and the work of teachers, are among those which are of more general current concern to teachers, administrators, advisers, governors and those involved in teacher education.

We are indebted to the heads and teachers of the schools in the survey without whose ready cooperation this report could not have been written.

As with other reports written by HMI, no assumption can be made about government commitment to the provision of additional resources as a result of the survey.

1 Introduction

THE DEVELOPMENT OF MIDDLE SCHOOLS

1.1 Middle schools are relatively new phenomena in the maintained education system in England. Their establishment was made possible by the Education Act of 1964 which enabled local education authorities to establish schools straddling primary and secondary age ranges. The first middle school opened in 1968 and thereafter there was a rapid expansion of middle school provision in a number of local education authorities until in January 1983 there were 1,810.[1] The age range of such schools varies from authority to authority and sometimes within an authority. Most often the schools are provided for children from the age of 9 to the age of 13 or from 8 to 12, but there are a few 9−12, 10−13 and 10−14 schools. Combined 5−12 schools have developed alongside 8−12 schools in some areas.

1.2 Under the 1964 Act middle schools are deemed to be either primary or secondary schools to comply with the provisions of the 1944 and subsequent Education Acts. All schools from which children transfer at the age of 12 are deemed primary and all but a very small number of schools from which children transfer at the age of 13 are deemed secondary. In January 1983 the total number of full-time pupils in 9−13 schools was 242,474 and those in 8−12 schools 210,051 ; approximately 22 per cent of eleven year olds in English maintained schools were in some type of middle school.[2] At the beginning of 1983, middle schools of one age range or another were found in 49 local education authorities.

1.3 The first middle schools were established in the late sixties when there were mounting pressures for the reorganisation of secondary education

---

[1] This includes 405 combined 5−12 schools.
[2] This includes children in combined 5−12 schools.

1

along non-selective lines and for the raising of the school leaving age to 16. In addition, there was considerable discussion about the age of transfer from primary to secondary education and about the most appropriate form of education to be provided for children in the middle years from 8 to 13. Both of these topics were examined by the report of the Central Advisory Council for Education (England) under the chairmanship of Lady Plowden (1967). In response to considerations such as these, some local education authorities adopted three-tier systems of first, middle and upper schools. In some areas there was a protracted period of reorganisation, resulting in some middle schools operating for a number of years with an age range other than that designated for them. Only a minority of schools could be provided with 'purpose-built' accommodation and most were therefore housed in ex-secondary or ex-primary premises, often adapted for middle school use.[1]

1.4 The period 1970–80 witnessed other developments which affected middle schools. In 1974 with the reorganisation of local government, some local education authorities disappeared, others were created, and many schools found themselves part of new administrative areas. In the mid-seventies there was increased public interest in the performance of the education system and the effects of economic restraint began to be felt. Towards the end of the period there was a growing concern about the likely consequences of contraction in pupil numbers. By the late seventies a considerable number of middle schools had been open for four or more years with a full age range. An appraisal of middle school education seemed timely, and plans were made to make a survey of 9–13 schools and, separately because of their different characteristics, of 8–12 and 5–12 schools. This report deals with the survey of 9–13 schools.

THE 9–13 MIDDLE SCHOOL SURVEY

1.5 Fifty 9–13 middle schools were chosen to illustrate a range of contexts. The survey set out to assess how well the schools provided for the age range and how well the children responded to the kind of education offered. In addition, it sought evidence about the general effects of school size and age range on the life and work of the schools.

1.6 Following a feasibility exercise in 1977 and a pilot exercise in spring 1979, the survey proper began in the autumn term 1979 and was almost completed

---

[1] See Appendix 1.

by the end of the summer term 1980. Inspections of 2 schools had to be held over. The schools inspected were some of the 360 which by the autumn term of 1979 had operated solely with a full 9–13 age range for four years or more. For the purposes of the survey, it was considered important to illustrate the diversity of school contexts within a sample whose size was constrained by the practical limitations on the number of schools which could be inspected. The schools selected illustrate this diversity but they are not a statistically representative sample of all such schools.[1] Thus, comment or quantification about the survey schools does not necessarily apply to all 9–13 middle schools.

1.7 Inspection teams were organised on a national basis and other arrangements were made which aimed to ensure a reasonable consistency of approach and comparability of standards. Each inspection team contained inspectors with particular knowledge of middle schools and experience of inspecting the 9–13 age range, as well as specialists in subject areas. Work was observed in all subjects normally included in the curriculum for the 9–13 age range in maintained schools, whether or not they were shown separately as subjects on the timetable. In addition to commenting upon the curriculum, inspectors also made observations about school organisation and management, pupils' social and personal development, and provision for children with special educational needs. Assessments of the work completed or in progress were based on the normal inspection methods of observation and discussion with teachers and pupils. Prior to the inspections the schools supplied a substantial amount of factual information about their organisation, finance, curriculum and staffing. This information provided the general context for discussion of the work observed. Inspection took place over a one-week period in larger middle schools but over a two-week period in smaller ones in an attempt not to overload the latter with visiting HMI. Between 10 and 13 inspectors were involved in each inspection to cover the general and subject-specific aspects of the school's work.

1.8 At the end of each inspection the customary discussion was held with the head, and usually a few weeks later, a meeting was held with the school governors. Following the procedure then in use a report on each individual school was issued to the head, the governors and the local education authority, but not published. Later, information received from schools and inspectors was collated and summarised to form the basis of this report.

---

[1] Appendix 1 gives details of the 48 schools visited.

1.9 The 9–13 middle school survey differed in important respects from both the primary and secondary surveys, and these differences are reflected in this report. Unlike *Primary education in England* (HMSO 1978) which examined aspects of the work of classes, this report discusses the life and work of entire schools. In contrast to *Aspects of secondary education in England* (HMSO 1979) which provided a detailed examination of language, mathematics, science, and personal and social development in the last 2 years of compulsory schooling, this report assesses the work undertaken by children aged 9 to 13 in a large number of subjects. Although dealing with more aspects of its sample schools than either the primary or the secondary survey, this document does not consider every important issue in the education of middle school pupils. For example, links between the home and the school, or between the school and the social services, are not discussed in any detail. Similarly, some issues have not been considered fully because of limitations of time and manpower. Continuity, for example, has been considered from the perspective of the middle schools but not from that of the first or upper schools. To do justice to the topic, work and procedures for continuity and liaison would have had to have been inspected in both the first and the upper schools – an impracticable task within the constraints of time and manpower operative at the time of the survey.

1.10 This report provides a 'snapshot' of the life and the work of 48 9–13 middle schools during a particular period ie the school year 1979–80. The report reveals a number of general and more subject-specific issues requiring consideration by those with an interest in the schools. As a result of developments since the survey was undertaken, the context for discussion of such issues has changed in some respects, the relative importance of some of the issues has altered, and other issues have come to the fore. The final chapter of the report includes discussion of more recent developments and their implications for 9–13 middle schools generally.

2 The main characteristics of the schools

2.1 This chapter provides an overall assessment of the life and work of the middle schools in the survey and makes some general suggestions as to how their work might further develop. In providing a composite picture, it cannot do justice to each one of the schools and it runs the risk of suggesting that practices within the schools were more uniform than was the case. Underlying most of the generalisations in this chapter were considerable variations from school to school and, sometimes, within schools.

2.2 The middle schools provided a broad range of subjects for their pupils. In each year group, children studied English, mathematics, science, music, religious education, physical education, arts and crafts, and aspects of humanities. Most of the older pupils were taught French and home studies, as were many younger ones.[1] The children applied themselves well to their tasks. They were taught a wide range of basic competencies but the schools often did not extend the work sufficiently to challenge their more able pupils nor were children often observed to be finding their own way to the solutions of problems posed, pursuing their own enquiries or making choices about the way in which the work was to be tackled. Although from time to time, in many schools, children studied aspects of the local environment, the amount of work involving first-hand experience was limited. Taking the schools as a whole, children were being introduced to a reasonably wide range of knowledge, skills and ideas, although within the curriculum studied, the schools showed a range and mixture of strengths and weaknesses. Detailed consideration of these variations is provided in Chapters 3 to 7 of this report. A few schools achieved good standards in almost all parts of the curriculum and a further third achieved generally satisfactory standards. In two-fifths of the schools work was judged to be fairly satisfactory, though within a wide range, where there were good levels of performance in some subjects and

---

[1] Paragraph 3.25.

5

where work was less than satisfactory in a number of others. In a small number of schools performance was considered less than adequate in most parts of the curriculum, often because the curriculum was too narrowly based and lacked extension.

2.3 Except in a very small number of schools where subject teaching was the predominant mode throughout, the schools provided a transition between class teaching and subject teaching.[1] In some, the transition was gradual so that, for example, the first year children were taught by their class teachers for most of the curriculum, the second year pupils were taught by class teachers for roughly two-thirds of the week, and the older pupils received largely subject teaching. A few schools provided a change in teaching mode at the beginning of the second year, when subject teaching was introduced for most of the curriculum ; in others, a marked change in mode occurred a year later. In a very small number of cases, class teaching predominated for the first three years, and a large element of subject teaching was introduced only for the oldest pupils.

2.4 The schools were orderly communities where the teachers placed great emphasis on the care and well-being of all pupils, not simply those who were experiencing problems. Relationships between the teachers and the children were characterised by friendliness, respect, concern and cooperation.[2] As they progressed through the schools, the children were helped by having regular contacts with form tutors or class teachers to whom they could turn for advice. The importance attached to personal relationships was shown also in the efforts made to consult parents about children's progress and problems, and to involve them in the day-to-day life of the schools.[3] Good relationships characterised schools in a wide variety of settings, and were not associated with any particular kind of catchment area.

2.5 For children in all year groups, but particularly the older ones, the life of the schools extended well beyond the timetabled day to include a range of clubs and societies meeting before and after school and during breaks.[4] Sporting activities, outdoor pursuits, clubs, residential visits, journeys abroad, and activities provided for the benefit of the local community contributed to children's personal and social development by using their interests and extending their capabilities further than was possible through timetabled lessons and by providing them with the chance to take

[1] Paragraphs 3.15–3.19
[2] Paragraph 4.2
[3] Paragraph 4.10–4.11
[4] Paragraph 4.7

responsibility, make decisions and exercise a degree of initiative. Many teachers devoted a considerable amount of their own time and energy to such activities, as did large numbers of children. The provision of voluntary activities was not confined to schools in particular social contexts. It was a valuable feature of the work of the schools generally and was an important factor in helping to create a sense of social cohesion and involvement.

THE CURRICULUM

2.6 With the exception of craft, design and technology which was not taught in nine of the sample, the schools offered a satisfactory range of subjects. In spite of their size, the 9 small[1] schools in the sample were able to offer a broad curriculum, although in three cases craft, design and technology was not provided. Within the 48 schools there was little variation in the range of subjects taught.[2] Where a subject was not included in the curriculum, for example craft, design and technology, this was usually due to lack of physical resources or the lack of suitably qualified or experienced teachers. Where this position is unlikely to be rectified in the short term, the schools should try to incorporate important elements of the omitted subjects into other areas of the curriculum. For example, the consideration of design problems need not be confined to work with resistant materials such as wood and metal but can be built into programmes of work in art.

2.7 In common with all schools, the middle schools had difficult decisions to make regarding the allocation of time to different parts of the curriculum. This was complicated by several factors such as the transition from class teaching to subject teaching, the introduction of additional subjects such as home studies, French, and craft, design and technology for many of the older pupils, and the constraints of subject teaching and accommodation. On average, most time was allocated to English and mathematics, although this decreased for the older pupils as new subjects were introduced into the

---

[1] For the purpose of the survey, the schools were divided into three broad size-bands based on the number of pupils on roll at the time of the inspections. The 9 schools, described here as 'small' schools, had fewer than 241 children on roll; the 25 'medium- size' schools had from 241 to 481 pupils, and the 14 'large' schools had over 480 on roll.

[2] Paragraph 3.25.

time-table.[1] In about two-thirds of the schools, the overall time allocated to subjects was judged to be reasonable. The remaining schools did not provide sufficient time for work to develop very far in range and depth in a number of subjects, very often music, or religious education, or arts and crafts.

2.8 Work was organised within separate subjects and within larger subject combinations such as design or social studies. Subject combinations were more common in the areas of humanities and arts and crafts than in other areas of the curriculum and were more likely to be provided for younger than older children.[2] Because of problems of time, accommodation, or the lack of enough appropriately qualified teachers, the majority of the schools made some use of rotational patterns where two or more subjects were time-tabled simultaneously for two or more classes and were each studied in turn by groups of children over a period of weeks or months. The subjects most often included in rotational patterns were art, home studies, needlecrafts, and craft, design and technology.[3] The survey did not reveal any clear connections between the quality of work and presence or absence of subject combinations or rotational patterns. Work of good quality was to be found in separate subjects, within subject combinations, and in rotational patterns.

2.9 Children were given adequate opportunities to practise the elementary skills of reading, writing and computation.[4] In some cases, too great an emphasis was placed on the practice of these skills at the expense of broader aspects of the work in English and mathematics. Compared with reading and writing, the importance of spoken language was often under-estimated.[5] In most of the schools children need more encouragement and opportunity to engage in extended discussion, where they can use language for a variety of purposes, such as to put forward arguments, to state generalisations, or to speculate about causes and motives.

2.10 Apart from the practice of the elementary skills there was considerable variation amongst the schools in terms of the range of work taught within subjects or areas of the curriculum. Details of these variations are discussed in Chapter 7 of this report. In a small number of schools, many of the teachers provided a wide range of learning activities ; children were expected to do

---

[1]On average 19 per cent of the teaching week was allocated to mathematics for the youngest pupils and 16 per cent for the oldest ones. English was timetabled for 25 per cent of the week for the younger children and 18 per cent of the week for the oldest ones.
[2]Paragraph 3.27
[3]Paragraph 3.28
[4]Paragraphs 7.12–7.13 and 7.29
[5]Paragraph 7.11

more than record and retain information or follow step-by-step instructions when practising skills ; they had, for example, to observe carefully, to solve problems, to offer generalisations or explanations, or to apply skills and ideas in new contexts. In such schools, teachers made effective use of a wide range of resources, such as the local environment, broadcasts, or museum loan services. In a few schools, children engaged in a limited range of activities in most areas of the curriculum. In most of the sample, however, the range of learning activities and resources used varied considerably from subject to subject. In general in the schools, an expansion of the range of resources and learning activities provided, including, in particular, the more effective use of the local environment, could help provide more opportunities for children to develop and display a variety of abilities.

2.11 The middle schools had schemes of work for most subjects.[1] These varied considerably in terms of their scope, their value, and the uses to which they were put. Some merely listed the topics to be dealt with and did not give adequate guidance on teaching approaches to be used or on progression in the work. The most useful schemes set out the scope of the subject matter to be taught, clarified the main ideas underlying the suggested content, discussed the skills children were to acquire, and suggested how progressively more demanding activities could be introduced. In most of the schools, teachers with designated curricular responsibilities[2] drew up the schemes, sometimes in consultation with other teachers involved in the teaching of the subject. In devising the schemes teachers often did not make sufficient use of guidance available, either from published material or from advisers or colleagues in other schools. More effective consultation inside and outside the school and greater awareness of guidance available in published form should help more of the schools to provide schemes of work or guidelines which take due account of the need for progression within the curriculum and which relate the tasks of teaching content and skills to the circumstances of the individual school, its resources, the opportunities presented by the local environment, and the expertise of the teachers.

2.12 The teachers made considerable efforts to assess and record the progress of individual children. Assessment took a variety of forms, varying from incidental day-to-day observations of children to formal procedures such as testing. In particular, teachers gave a great deal of attention to assessing work in English[3] and mathematics[4] through the periodic use of

---

[1] Paragraph 6.3
[2] Paragraph 6.2
[3] Paragraph 6.6
[4] Paragraph 6.7

standardised tests and internally devised examinations as well as the marking of children's work. In many cases, the range of cirteria used in marking was rather narrow and needed to be widened to include consideration of, for example, the quality of reasoning and the methods used by children in tackling problems in mathematics, or the clarity, style and content of communication in written English. The schools would profit by trying to make explicit the criteria used to judge children's work in different areas of the curriculum and by drawing up agreed marking policies about the scales or grades to be used. In many of the schools, the function of assessment and record-keeping should be widened to include the diagnosis of individual pupils' difficulties as a basis for planning work to remedy these and as a means of providing teachers with information about the suitability of the work being undertaken by the children.[1]

2.13 Almost all the schools provided both boys and girls with a similar range of opportunities, within the curriculum and in the wider life of the schools. Boys and girls usually followed the same courses and shared in activities such as woodwork, cooking and needlecrafts. In a number of cases, they were taught separately for some subjects in some year groups, or allocated different amounts of time for subjects such as home studies or craft, design and technology. In the 4 schools where similar opportunities were not provided for boys and girls it was suggested that existing curricular arrangements needed to be reviewed as a matter of priority.

2.14 Children were taught in mixed-ability classes for most subjects in most of the schools. Only 2 schools streamed children according to ability throughout the age range but 7 streamed pupils in the third year and 12 in the fourth year. More frequently, setting was used as a way of organising ability groups of older children for the teaching of mathematics, French, English, and to a lesser extent science. First year children were set by ability for mathematics in 19 schools, and second year children in 31.[2].

2.15 Whatever the ability group, the content and pace of work and the teaching approaches used were most often directed towards the children of average ability in a class. Less often were objectives, methods or materials differentiated to cater for the full range of children's capabilities. In particular, not enough demands were made on the more able minority, who were usually not given the chance to work in sufficient depth to produce material of high quality. Compared with the more able, the less able were better provided for

[1]Paragraphs 6.14–6.15
[2]Paragraph 3.22

and more often given work which took due account of their difficulties, although in some subjects, eg mathematics, the range of work was often restricted and the content unappealing. Children across the ability range were more likely to receive appropriately demanding work in mathematics, English and science, where setting was commonly used, than in other subjects.[1]

2.16 In general, the children responded positively to the tasks set by teachers as part of the formal curriculum and, even more so, to the range of voluntary activities provided by the school.[2] Pupils were well behaved, industrious, and willing to assume responsibility, to make choices and to exercise initiative.[3] Their ready response suggested that the schools could valuably extend the range of such opportunities, particularly during lesson time, where very often the work was closely directed by the teacher and offered insufficient scope for individuals or groups of children to put forward their own ideas, pursue their own questions, or exercise choice from a number of possibilities.

LIAISON

2.17 Most of the middle schools recognised the importance of liaison with first and upper schools to help provide continuity in the teaching for children as they moved from one school to another. Liaison took two main forms: the transfer of information about individual pupils and consultation about the curriculum. Commendable efforts were made to ease the transfer of children from one school to the next.[4] The middle schools found continuity difficult to achieve when they had to consult with a considerable number of first and upper schools. Few had only one or two first schools and one upper school with which they had to consult. About half the schools each received children from more than five first schools, and just under half transferred pupils to four or more upper schools.[5]

2.18 Information about the progress of individual children was normally passed on from the first to the middle and from the middle to the upper school, and steps were taken to familiarise children with the schools to which they were transferring. Contacts between first and middle school teachers

---

[1] The appropriateness of the work in specific subjects is discussed in the various sub-sections of Chapter 7.
[2] Paragraph 4.3
[3] Paragraphs 4.4—4.6
[4] Paragraphs 6.17, 6.18, 6.21
[5] Paragraph 6.16

11

were common but tended to be limited to the consideration of mathematics, reading, and the problems of children in need of special help.[1] There appeared to be little emphasis on the coordination of other areas of the curriculum at this stage. Many of the teachers met with colleagues from other middle schools and from upper schools to discuss the content of the curriculum, especially in French, mathematics, science and English.[2] However, there was considerable variation among the schools in the range of topics included in their courses and in the proportion of their pupils to whom these topics were taught. The contacts already established between the middle schools and others in their localities need to be strengthened even further and greater efforts made to achieve more consistent coverage, especially where a number of middle schools send children to the same upper school. Effective contacts among the middle schools and between them and the upper schools should make it possible for teachers in upper schools to plan work for their youngest pupils which enable the latter to proceed with the minimum of disruption to their studies.[3]

STAFFING

2.19 Just under half of the teachers in the survey schools had taken either junior-secondary or middle years courses of initial training, and almost all the remainder had taken courses preparing them to teach in either primary or secondary schools.[4] Most had more than 5 years teaching experience and almost two-thirds had been at the same middle school for 4 years or more.[5] One in 4 of the teachers were graduates of whom just under half had taken Bachelor of Education degrees.[6] The average pupil-teacher ratio for the schools was 20.2 :1, but the ratio for individual schools ranged from 13.2 :1 to 24.6 :1. In general, the small schools had more favourable pupil-teacher ratios than the larger ones.[7] In addition to their permanent staff, almost all the schools had the services of peripatetic or visiting teachers, usually for instrumental music tuition or, in some cases, for help with remedial work.[8]

---

[1] Paragraphs 6.18, 6.19
[2] Paragraphs 6.20, 6.22
[3] Paragraph 6.23
[4] Appendix 1 Paragraph 6
[5] Appendix 1 Paragraph 10
[6] Appendix 1 Paragraph 5
[7] Appendix 2 Paragraph 12
[8] Appendix 1 Paragraph 13

2.20 Except in a very small number of schools where subject teaching was the predominant mode throughout, the schools employed a 'mixed economy' of class and subject teaching.[1] This 'mixed economy' made it comparatively rare for a teacher to be deployed solely to teach one subject, though this did not prevent about a third of the teachers from concentrating for over half of their time on one particular aspect of the curriculum.[2] In contrast, many teachers, particularly those who had been trained for primary or middle years teaching, were able to cover a range of subjects with the younger children. Overall, the vast majority of the teachers taught several subjects to one or more year groups. About two-thirds taught some English, a similar proportion taught aspects of humanities and over half some mathematics.[3]

2.21 As with primary and some secondary school teachers, most of the middle school teachers taught a wider range of subjects than they themselves had studied as main subjects in their initial training. In such circumstances, it was important that they had easy access to advice from colleagues who had studied the subjects concerned. Almost all the schools had teachers who could offer advice about science, English, humanities, art and craft, physical education, mathematics and French respectively. However, a considerable number of the schools did not have teachers who had studied one of the following as a main subject : music, home studies, religious education, or craft, design and technology.[4]

2.22 In deploying their staff, heads took into consideration the subjects taken by teachers during initial training, as well as the range of their subsequent teaching experience and the in-service courses they had attended. Within the constraints posed by the staffing levels in the schools, considerable efforts were made to capitalise on the strengths and interests of teachers. Thus, of those teachers who spent over half their week teaching a particular subject, three-quarters or more had studied it as a main subject during initial training in the cases of art, history, georgraphy, science, music, physical education, French and home studies. For English and mathematics, which took up a substantially greater proportion of time-tabled time and involved more teachers, the percentage of such teachers who had studied them as main subjects was 70 per cent and 60 per

[1]Paragraphs 3.15–3.18
[2]Paragraph 3.14
[3]Paragraph 3.13
[4]Appendix 1 Paragraph 7

cent respectively.[1] The older the children, the more likely they were to receive subject teaching from staff who taught the subject for a considerable proportion of their week and who had studied it during initial training.

2.23 The assessments made of work in the schools were analysed to see if there were any significant associations between particular modes of staff deployment and overall standards.[2] For the purposes of analysis, two methods were used to assess the degree to which subject teaching was employed in the schools. One was concerned with the proportion of teachers who spent over half their week teaching one specific subject; the other, with the proportion of the teaching in the schools which was undertaken by teachers who had studied the subjects they taught as main subjects in initial training. In both cases, there was a statistically significant association between a greater degree of subject teaching and better standards of work.

2.24 The head's role was of particular importance in providing general direction for the work of the schools, in monitoring developments, and in exercising oversight of the deployment of staff, the planning of the time-table, and the supply of resources. Standards of work were higher in those schools where the heads were a strong influence.[3]

2.25 Though retaining general oversight of the curriculum and teaching arrangements heads delegated responsibility for aspects of the schools' work. In each school, there was a number of teachers with designated curricular responsibilities. Their duties normally included the preparation of schemes of work, the provision of advice to colleagues, and the coordination of work in their subject throughout the school. Most such teachers spent a considerable proportion of their week teaching their subject; about three-quarters of those staff who spent over half their week teaching a subject had designated responsibility for the subject concerned. On average, teachers with curricular responsibilities had only just over three hours per week when they were not time-tabled to teach and when they were expected to carry out their additional responsibilities.[4] Where the necessary support was given by heads and other senior staff, such teachers were able to have a strong influence on the quality of the work by, for example, involving colleagues in cooperative planning, by working alongside teachers in the classroom, by identifying needs for in-service training, and, in particular, by demonstrating through personal example what could be achieved. Especially in the cases of

---

[1]Tables 4 and 5
[2]Paragraph 3.19 and Appendix 2 Paragraphs 7–8
[3]Paragraph 3.2 and Appendix 2 Paragraphs 7–8
[4]Paragraph 3.8

English and mathematics, teachers with designated curricular responsibilities tended to be deployed solely in teaching the older age groups, but
there were examples of very good work being done by such teachers with the
younger children. The schools should consider whether there is advantage in
such teachers teaching in a number of year groups to provide them with an
overview of the work being done throughout the school, and in their teaching
classes or groups of less able children to help them provide guidance to other
teachers about the problems their subjects present to such children. In order
to provide support for colleagues, teachers with designated curricular
responsibilities need opportunities to keep themselves up-to-date with
teaching approaches, materials and modes of assessment used in their
subjects. They also need to meet regularly with teachers holding similar
responsibilities in other schools to help provide continuity of experience for
children as they transfer from first to middle and from middle to upper
schools.

2.26 In most of the schools heads also delegated responsibility for the
planning and supervision of work within year groups.[1] Coordinators
undertook this task which also involved the organisation of teaching groups,
the day-to-day management of resources, and the pastoral care of children
within the year group. Many coordinators helped to promote a systematic
approach to the teaching of children in their year group, but too great an
emphasis on the year group did sometimes have disadvantages. In some
cases, the curriculum and teaching approaches lacked adequate continuity
from year to year because of the undue emphasis given to the autonomy of
separate year groups.

2.27 Particularly, but not only in small schools, a considerable number of
teachers held both organisational and curricular responsibilities or had
oversight of two areas of the curriculum. In many cases, the demands made
on such teachers were very considerable.[2]

2.28 The discharge of organisational or curricular responsibilities required
time both in and outside normal school hours. Some aspects of organisation
and planning were carried out in out-of-school hours but the provision of
effective professional leadership and support requires time to be made

---

[1]Paragraph 3.7
[2]Paragraphs 3.7 and 3.9

available during the school day. The time provided was insufficient in most cases. In very many of the schools, teachers with responsibilities need more time during the school day to observe the work children in other classes are doing and to guide and support other members of staff.

ACCOMMODATION AND RESOURCES[1]

2.29 Most of the schools were either in premises adapted for middle school use or in purpose-built accommodation. Just under a quarter were housed in ex-secondary accommodation where no adaptations had been made to cater for the new age range of pupils.[2] In the light of the range of work being attempted, the accommodation was judged to be generally satisfactory in two-thirds of the schools, including a quarter where the provision of specialist and general teaching rooms was considered good.[3] In the remaining third, facilities for several subjects were not considered adequate. Most of the schools in the survey had designated teaching areas for science, physical education, home studies, arts and crafts, and music.[4] In general, the older the children the more likely they were to be taught in designated teaching areas, but many first and second year pupils had access to specialised facilities for science and practical subjects. Many schools did not have appropriate teaching spaces for small groups withdrawn from classes for remedial work, and a large number lacked adequate storage facilities for some subjects such as home studies, science, art and design, or craft, design and technology. A fair proportion did not have appropriate changing rooms.

2.30 In about two-thirds of the schools, the overall level of resources was considered to be adequate for most of the work being undertaken, but in only ten of these was provision judged to be generally good.[5] Overall, the small schools did not have significantly poorer resources than the large ones.[6] An analysis of the overall assessments made of general standards of work achieved in each subject in each school indicated that better quality and greater quantities of material resources were significantly associated with higher standards of work.[7] In general, the schools were less well supplied with books than with equipment. Although there was adequate book provision for mathematics, modern languages, English and history respectively in about

---

[1]Throughout the report the term 'resources' refers to material resources, for example books, equipment and apparatus, consumable materials.
[2]Appendix 1 Paragraph 16
[3]Details of accommodation for specific subjects are given in Chapter 7 and in Appendix 1.
[4]Appendix 1 Paragraph 20
[5]Details of resources for specific subjects are given in Chapter 7 and in Appendix 1
[6]Appendix 1 Paragraph 25
[7]Appendix 1 Paragraph 29

two-thirds of the schools, other subjects were less well supplied; in particular, in about two-thirds of the schools, stocks of books were not adequate for the work in religious education. A similar proportion of the schools lacked satisfactory reference books for art, needlecrafts, physical education, or craft, design and technology. In contrast, equipment was satisfactory in quality and quantity for the work being undertaken in each area of the curriculum in at least three-fifths of the schools.[1]

STANDARDS OF WORK

2.31 On the basis of HMI's experience of work undertaken by children of comparable age in other schools nationwide, overall assessments of standards were made in the light of each school's circumstances. Five of the 48 schools, including one with social priority status, were judged to be achieving good standards in most parts of the curriculum. In these schools, the work was generally well planned and showed an awareness of the need for progression from the first year to the fourth. Teachers used a variety of teaching methods and provided a range of activities which were well presented and organised and to which the children responded with interest. Attempts were being made, not always successfully, to provide appropriate work for the full range of children's abilities. A third of the survey schools were judged to be achieving generally satisfactory standards, with good levels of performance in some areas, acceptable levels in others and only the occasional subject where work was less than satisfactory. In about two-fifths of the schools, standards were much more uneven, with good work in some areas but unsatisfactory work in others. In only six of the schools were standards of work judged to be unsatisfactory in most areas of the curriculum, although in these schools examples of good work were seen in some subjects. In general, the standards of work achieved in the small schools were comparable with those achieved in the medium-sized schools. However, the large schools which had over 480 pupils on roll achieved rather higher standards generally than the schools with fewer pupils.[2]

2.32 Overall, standards were most often judged to be satisfactory or better in mathematics, English and science. Work was least often satisfactory in geography, religious education and needlecrafts, although in each of these subjects good standards were achieved in a small number of the schools. More detailed consideration of the standards, scope and content of the work in each subject is provided in Chapter 7 of this report.

[1]Appendix 1 Paragraph 27
[2]Appendix 2 Paragraphs 7 and 8

3 The management and organisation of the teaching arrangements

THE HEADS

3.1 The heads of the middle schools, through consultation with senior staff, made decisions about the allocation of responsibilities, the deployment of staff, the composition of classes and teaching groups, and the timetabling arrangements. Each of these is discussed later in this chapter.

3.2 The heads varied in their approaches to managing their schools, but overall, standards of work were higher in those schools where the heads provided positive leadership through assessing what was being done, considering whether changes in direction or emphasis were needed, consulting staff about possible changes and delegating responsibility, where desirable, for the implementation of decisions. These heads commanded the respect of the teachers and children by their own skill in teaching, and their expectations of high standards of work and behaviour. They established effective links with parents and the local community. In one school, for example, which was in a socially disadvantaged area, the head, who had been in his post for more than twenty years, had been the major influence in creating high standards of work across the curriculum and in enlisting the support of parents who, among other things, had made book and display shelves, and raised funds to help build an indoor swimming pool and equip the drama studio with a movie camera and a video recorder.

3.3 Although the heads of the schools in the survey necessarily spent a good deal of time on administrative matters – meeting parents, dealing with visitors, routine administration and other, not always predictable, demands – almost all of them taught classes or groups of children on a regular basis, most frequently for English, mathematics, religious education or remedial work. On average, heads taught for about a quarter of the teaching week ; heads of 'small' schools tended to teach for a rather larger proportion of the week than their counterparts in larger schools. This teaching commitment often helped the head to get to know the children and their levels of attainment. In eight schools, heads took on special responsibilities for specific areas of the curriculum in addition to their more general responsibilities.

THE ALLOCATION OF RESPONSIBILITIES

3.4 Typically the heads allocated responsibilities to their deputies, to teachers responsible for coordinating the work of year groups, and to those responsible for coordinating the work in specific subjects or areas of the curriculum.

3.5 Thirty seven of the schools had one deputy head and 10, the larger ones, had two. Deputy heads carried out the responsibilities of heads in their absence and were usually involved in the day-to-day administration of the schools. They were often responsible for requisitioning stock, for drawing up the timetable and for keeping it under review throughout the year. Most had responsibilities for pastoral care, in some cases a particular concern for either girls' or boys' welfare. The supervision of probationary teachers and liaison with tutors concerning students on teaching practice were frequently part of their duties. Examples were seen of deputies influencing the work through good teaching, efficient administration, support for less experienced staff, and effective display of children's work. Over three-quarters of deputies held curricular responsibilities in addition to their organisational ones. On average, deputy heads had about seven hours a week when they were not timetabled to teach and in which they were expected to carry out their additional responsibilities.[1]

3.6 Some schools were large enough to employ a teacher on a senior teacher's scale. Very often, senior teachers took responsibility for pastoral care – usually for either boys' or girls' welfare. Some undertook administrative tasks such as the ordering of materials or the oversight of school records. In some cases, they were involved in the supervision of probationary teachers and students and in liaison with colleges and institutes of higher education. Twenty eight members of staff in the schools visited

---

[1] On average, deputy heads of 'large' schools had about $9\frac{1}{4}$ hours for carrying out other responsibilities ; in 'medium-sized' schools 7 hours and in 'small' schools $5\frac{1}{2}$ hours.

were designated as senior teachers ; all of them were in 'medium-sized' or 'large' schools. On average, senior teachers had about 5 hours a week to carry out their additional responsibilities.[1] Twenty senior teachers had responsibilities for subjects or areas of the curriculum.

3.7 In 41 of the schools there were teachers who had responsibilities for the work of particular year groups. The most common arrangement was to deploy a coordinator for each of the year groups. They normally combined the planning and supervision of work within the year group with responsibility for pastoral care, which sometimes involved consultations with parents and others such as educational welfare officers. Coordinators were usually responsible for the organisation of teaching within their year group, the management of resources, the testing of pupils, and the maintenance of records of children's progress. They normally had general oversight of the work of their year group including such activities as educational visits and year assemblies. They were expected to consult with other year-group coordinators within the school and with teachers having special responsibilities for subjects or areas of the curriculum. Thirty had specific responsibilities for liaison with first schools and a similar number for liaison with upper schools. On average, year-group coordinators had about three hours of the school week to carry out their additional responsibilities. About 70 per cent of them had at least one curricular responsibility, which they exercised in addition to their other duties. This made heavy demands on the individuals concerned. Although there were advantages in year-group co-ordinators also having the responsibility to review the work in a subject throughout the school, the small amount of time allowed for carrying out these duties limited what could be achieved.

3.8 In most cases, one teacher was responsible for coordinating work in a subject throughout the school, but in some schools, this responsibility was shared. The work of such teachers normally included the preparation of schemes of work and the coordination of the teaching of the subject. Many acted as consultants, giving advice to other teachers when requested. In many schools, they were responsible for the allocation of resources for their subject and for liaison with teachers of the subject in other schools. Teachers with responsibility for physical education and for music were most often involved in the organisation of extra-curricular activities. The large majority of schools had teachers with special curricular responsibility in mathematics, French, science, music, physical education and English (see Table 1). In most cases these teachers had studied the subjects as main subjects in their initial

[1] On average, senior teachers in 'medium-sized' schools had 4¼ hours for other responsibilities ; in 'large' schools 6½ hours.

training. In all, just over half of the teachers in the survey had special curricular responsibilities ; the average time allowed these teachers for their additional duties was 3¼ hours per week. About a quarter of these teachers had oversight of two curricular areas or subjects. Despite the limited time available for these additional duties many teachers were making a successful contribution in maintaining oversight of the progress in their subject or subjects.

3.9 In all, just over a quarter of the teachers in the schools held both organisational and curricular responsibilities. Over three-fifths of the deputy heads and teachers on scale 3 held both types of responsibility, as did over a quarter of the teachers on scale 2. The proportion of teachers holding both types of responsibility was greatest in the small schools.[1] In many cases the teachers were not given sufficient time during the teaching week to carry out these demanding responsibilities.

3.11 Where teachers with special responsibilities were given clear guidance as to the nature of these responsibilities and how they were to be carried out they were more effective in influencing the work and conduct of the school. Only about a third of the heads in the survey provided written job specifications ; where this was done it assisted both the postholder and other teachers.

THE DEPLOYMENT OF TEACHERS

3.12 Many factors in addition to the size of the school and the number of teachers influenced the way the heads deployed their teaching staff. These included the heads' view of the middle school, the organisation of the curriculum, the type and size of teaching groups, the utilisation of the skills and backgrounds of teachers, and the time made available in school hours for other professional duties. All these factors were interrelated and decisions about one were likely to affect the others. This section provides an overview of staff deployment in the forty-eight schools at the time of the survey. Underlying the general features discussed here there were considerable variations within the sample arising from the unique circumstances of each of the schools.

---

[1] 43 per cent of teachers in 'small' schools and 30 per cent of teachers in 'medium-sized' schools held both organisational and curricular responsibilities, as did 22 per cent of teachers in the 'large' schools.

3.13 Table 2 shows how many teachers in the schools were involved in broad areas of the curriculum such as humanities and arts and crafts and in particular subjects such as music or home studies. The broad areas of arts and crafts, humanities, modern languages, English and physical education are sub-divided into constituent subjects in Table 3, which shows the number of teachers teaching each of these subjects. Overall, about two-thirds of the teachers taught some English, a similar proportion taught some aspects of humanities and over half some mathematics.

3.14 Most of the teachers taught a number of different subjects, often to children in more than one year group. Some, especially those trained for primary or middle years teaching, taught a wide range of subjects to first or second year children. However, almost a third of the teachers were able to spend over half their time teaching one specific subject. Of these, 70 per cent had a special curricular responsibility for the subject (Table 4), and 66 per cent had studied the subject as a main subject in their initial training or as part of their degree (Table 5).[1] In the cases of science, music, French, physical education, geography and history, 80 per cent or more of those who spent over half their time teaching the subject had studied it as a main subject in initial training.

3.15 The patterns of teaching typically used in the middle schools differed somewhat from those used in primary or secondary schools. In primary schools, class teachers are normally responsible for teaching the major part of the curriculum of their classes, although over three-quarters of all classes in the national primary survey were taught for some time during the week by teachers other than their own class teachers, excluding peripatetic teachers. In secondary schools, pupils are normally taught by a number of specialist teachers who spend much of the week teaching their own particular subjects, though in some schools, younger secondary pupils are taught by considerably fewer specialists than older ones. The middle schools contained children of both primary and secondary age and the great majority of them provided a transition from predominantly class teaching for their youngest children to predominantly subject teaching for the oldest. In most of the

---

[1] The analysis of subjects studied by teachers (Table 5) was based on information from heads' questionnaires. Teachers were asked to name the subject (or subjects) they had studied :

a) as part of their first degree
b) as a main subject for their BEd degree
c) as a main subject for their teaching certificate.

51 per cent named one subject only ; 39 per cent named two subjects ; 10 per cent named three subjects. No information was collected about the subsidiary or supporting subjects studied by teachers.

schools, irrespective of size, children in the first year were taught mainly by the class teacher and as they progressed through the school, they were increasingly taught by subject teachers so that by the fourth year the curriculum was largely organised along subject teaching lines. Apart from this overall trend, Table 6 shows two particular changes of emphasis : one from the first to the second year when there was a large increase in the number of classes taught by the class teacher and separate subject teachers and the other from the second to the third year when there was a marked increase in the number of classes where most subjects were taught by separate subject teachers. Through a variety of patterns of staff deployment, most of the schools moved from a predominantly primary organisation based on one class teacher for most of the curriculum to a predominantly secondary organisation based on the use of separate subject teachers.

3.16 To illustrate the variety of ways in which this was satisfactorily achieved, three examples are given here. In one school with over 500 children on roll, all the first year children were taught in mixed ability groups, mainly by their respective class teachers. In the second year about half of the work was carried out by class teachers and there was setting for mathematics. The third year pupils were largely taught by a number of subject teachers and setting was employed for English and mathematics. The fourth year children were also taught in the main by a number of subject teachers with setting in English, mathematics and science.

3.17 In a second school, with just over 120 children on roll, first and second year pupils were taught in mixed ability classes and remained with their class teachers for English, mathematics, religious education and topic work. For the other subjects they were taught by the respective subject teachers in specialist accommodation. In the third and fourth years each year group was divided into two separate class groups based on ability and each was taught by subject teachers, usually in specialist accommodation.

3.18 In a third school, which catered for over 600 children, the first year children were taught in five mixed ability classes, mainly by their class teachers, although there was some use of specialist subject teachers for French and physical education and, to a lesser extent, for music and science. Second, third and fourth year pupils were arranged in five classes within each year and taught by subject teachers.

3.19 Statistical analysis was used to see if there were any significant associations between the degree of use of subject teaching in the schools and overall standards of work. Two methods were used to assess the degree of use of subject teaching used in the schools. One referred to the proportion of teachers who spent over half their time teaching one specific subject ; the other, to the proportion of teaching which was undertaken by teachers who had studied the subjects they taught as main subjects in initial training. In both cases, higher standards of work overall were associated with a greater degree of use of subject teachers.

THE COMPOSITION OF CLASSES AND TEACHING GROUPS

3.20 In all of the schools, decisions had to be made as to whether to arrange classes so that they contained children born in the same school year or whether they should have children from two or more age groups. At the time of the survey none of the schools arranged the majority of its classes in mixed age groups. In all, only three classes contained substantial numbers of children from each of two year groups. These were found in two of the schools, but in a further nine, there were one or two classes with a majority of children from one year group and a small number from a different one. In the remaining schools, all registration classes contained children from one year group only.

3.21 The second factor which the heads took into account when arranging classes was the ability of the children. They had to decide whether to form mixed-ability classes containing pupils of widely different abilities or whether to sub-divide the whole ability range within year groups. Where the latter course of action was decided upon, many heads regrouped children into sets according to their ability in specific subjects ; some heads assigned pupils to streamed classes on some overall assessment of general ability ; a few adopted banding and divided the year groups into two or more bands differentiated by ability and containing a number of parallel classes. Within many of the schools, a variety of pupil groupings was employed, depending on the age of the children and the subjects they were being taught.

3.22 Most of the survey schools formed mixed-ability classes for the majority of subjects. But, as Table 7 shows, most of the schools made some use of setting for a small number of subjects, more often with older pupils and in respect of English, mathematics and French. Only 2 schools streamed children according to ability throughout the age range, but 7 streamed children in the third year and 12 in the fourth year. In 2 schools, banding was employed in all four year groups : this form of organisation was used in 7 schools in the third year and in 4 in the fourth year.

24

3.23 Almost every school made arrangements to give extra help to children who found reading and writing particularly difficult. In two-thirds of the schools, such children were taught in groups withdrawn from some of the classes. This arrangement was more frequently made for first and second year pupils than for older ones. Six schools had designated remedial classes in which children spent most of the school week. Less often were special arrangements made for those children considered very able, though some schools withdrew individuals or groups and a few employed supernumerary teachers to work with such pupils.

TIMETABLING ARRANGEMENTS

3.24 In the light of local education authority policies, and other factors, heads and teachers had to make decisions about the timetable – the subjects or areas of the curriculum to be included, the amount of time to be devoted to each subject per week, the distribution of time in terms of single, double or more extended periods, and the number and kinds of teaching groups for which time had to be allocated. Arrangements also had to be made for the particular skills of teachers to be properly available throughout the school to pupils and other teachers. In an attempt to provide appropriately for each subject or area, schools adopted one or more timetabling devices. Some of the schools provided one or more periods of time per week for each separate subject ; usually, the different time requirements of subjects were taken into account so that, for example, practical subjects were given larger blocks of time than subjects such as French or religious education. Some of the schools grouped two or more subjects together on the timetable to form combinations such as humanities or design, which were offered to all or some children. In order to avoid small weekly allocations of time or because of problems of accommodation or staff deployment, some schools made use of rotational patterns where two or more subjects were timetabled simultaneously for two or more classes and were each studied in turn by groups of children over a period of weeks or months. In some cases, areas such as health education were not timetabled separately but were intended to influence the nature of the work in different subjects and provided a means of interrelating work in different parts of the curriculum. Each of these arrangements, or combinations of arrangements, had accompanying advantages and disadvantages. In reaching decisions about timetabling arrangements, the individual schools had to take into account the overall organisation of their curriculum, their staffing, accommodation and resources, and the number and distribution of children in each year group and their various aptitudes and needs. There was no one set of timetabling arrangements that was appropriate for all the schools.

3.25 In each school, the timetable included English, mathematics, physical education, religious education, art and design, music, science, French and aspects of history and geography. Science was taught to first year children in 46 schools and to second, third and fourth year pupils in all schools. French was part of the curriculum for most third and fourth year children in every school and for most second year children in 45 ; it was taught to many of the youngest children in just over half the sample. In almost every school, home studies was timetabled for third and fourth year pupils and was provided for second year children in over two-thirds of the schools and for first year children in half the sample. Aspects of craft, design and technology were taught to older pupils in 39 schools and were provided for younger children in about half the sample. Needlecrafts were taught to the younger children in about three-quarters of the schools and to older pupils in almost every school.

3.26 Although there were considerable variations among the schools in the amount of time given to particular subjects, the two subjects allocated most time overall in each year group were English and mathematics and usually these two subjects were timetabled every day. On average English was timetabled for 25 per cent of the week for the younger children and for 18 per cent of the week for the oldest ones. Mathematics took up about 19 per cent of the time for the youngest and 16 per cent for the oldest pupils. In each year group, about 16 per cent of the time was devoted to aspects of humanities, which in some schools were timetabled as subject combinations and in others as separate subjects. Throughout all four years about 10 per cent of the time was allocated to physical education and a similar proportion to French and to arts and crafts. The percentage of the time devoted to science increased from about 6 per cent for first year pupils to 10 per cent for fourth year children. Home studies and music each took up slightly under 5 per cent of the week on average.

3.27 In three-fifths of the schools, the timetable for each of the four year groups included subject combinations, mainly in the area of humanities and to a lesser extent in arts and crafts. Subject combinations were provided in forty-three schools for at least some younger children and in thirty-six schools for some older pupils.

3.28 Two-thirds of the schools reported that parts of their timetables were organised on a rotational basis. The subjects most often included in the rotational patterns were art, home studies, needlecrafts, and craft, design and technology. This organisation was designed to ensure that each pupil covered the same range of studies within the year. The nature of the practical activities and, in some cases, safety factors meant there was advantage in reorganising the registration classes into smaller groups for this work. In 19 schools, rotational patterns were used in all four year groups and in a further 8 schools, in all but the first year. The percentage of time in the week allocated to rotational patterns varied from 2.5 per cent to 20 per cent. Most patterns were organised on a termly or half-termly basis.

3.29 Analysis of the survey's findings did not reveal any direct associations between the quality of the work and the presence or absence of subject combinations or rotational patterns.

ANNEX TO CHAPTER 3

Table 1 *Number of schools having teachers with special curricular responsibilities — by subject*

Subject	Number of schools
Mathematics	48
French	46
Science	46
Music	45
Physical education	45
English	42
Art and design	38
Home studies	34
Remedial teaching	31
Religious education	30
History	23
Craft, design and technology	22
Geography	20
Drama	15
Needlecrafts	15
Humanities	11
Social studies	9
Environmental studies	8
Health education	7
Rural studies	5
English as a second language	2
Dance	1
Other foreign language	1

Table 2 *The number of teachers teaching curricular areas or subjects*

Curricular areas or subjects	Number of teachers teaching the curricular area or subject*
Humanities**	684
English**	677
Mathematics	579
Physical education**	458
Arts and crafts**	390
Science	258
Remedial work	203
Music	201
Modern languages**	191
Home studies	68
Rural studies	15
Number of teachers in the sample	1003

* The total number of teachers in this column exceeds the total number of teachers in the sample, since most of the teachers taught more than one subject.

**Teachers taught one or more of the constituent subjects in the curricular area.

Table 3 *The number of teachers teaching constituent subjects of curricular areas*

Curricular areas	Subjects	Number of teachers teaching the subject
Humanities*	History	123
	Geography	126
	Religious education	354
	Environmental studies	121
	Social Studies	134
	Humanities	193
English*	English	673
	Drama	58
Arts and Crafts*	Art and design	297
	Craft, design and technology	96
	Needlecrafts	38
Physical education*	Physical education	454
	Dance	18
Modern languages*	French	185
	other modern foreign languages	6

Number of teachers in the sample = 1003.

*Teachers taught one or more of the constituent subjects in the curricular area.

Table 4 *Deployment of teachers with curricular responsibilities*

Subject	Number of teachers teaching the subject	Number teaching the subject for 51% or more of their week	Number of teachers with a special curricular res- ponsibility	Number with a special curricular responsibility and teaching the subject for 51% or more of their week
English	673	33	59	18
Art and design	297	20	46	11
Craft, design and technology	96	16	28	10
Religious education	354	6	34	4
History	123	5	25	4
Geography	126	5	21	4
Science	258	39	54	30
Mathematics	579	35	60	23
Music	201	16	54	13
Physical education	454	28	75	24
Dance	18	0	1	0
Drama	58	1	15	1
French	185	31	51	27
Other modern languages	6	0	1	1
Social studies	134	0	9	0
Environmental studies	121	2	12	1
Rural studies	15	1	5	0
Humanities	193	6	14	4
Home studies	68	23	36	17
Needlecrafts	38	2	16	1
Remedial teaching	203	32	39	17
		301		210

Table 5 *Deployment of teachers — by subject*

Subject	Number of teachers teaching the subject	Number teaching who studied the subject as part of a first degree or as a main subject in their certificate	Number teaching who studied the subject as part of a first degree or as a main subject in their certificate and teaching it for 51% or more of their week
English	673	195	23
Art and design	297	77	15
Craft, design and technology	96	22	7
Religious education	354	39	3
History	123	44	5
Geography	126	46	4
Science	258	94	32
Mathematics	579	110	21
Music	201	57	13
Physical education	454	95	27
Dance	18	1	0
Drama	58	6	0
French	185	68	28
Other modern languages	6	1	1
Social studies	134	2	0
Environmental studies	121	5	0
Rural studies	15	3	0
Humanities	193	2	0
Home studies	68	33	18
Needlecrafts	38	9	0
Remedial teaching	203	3	3

Table 6 *Heads' classification of their forms of year group organisation*

	1–240	241 –480	481 +	TOTAL
	Size Range			
	NUMBER OF SCHOOLS			
Organisation				
First year classes				
Mainly subject specialist	2	0	1	3
Mainly class teacher	6	24	10	40
Subject specialist + class teacher	1	1	3	5
Second year classes				
Mainly subject specialist	3	0	3	6
Mainly class teacher	3	15	4	22
Subject specialist + class teacher	3	10	7	20
Third year classes				
Mainly subject specialist	7	13	11	31
Mainly class teacher	0	1	1	2
Subject specialist + class teacher	2	11	2	15
Fourth year classes				
Mainly subject specialist	8	20	12	40
Mainly class teacher	0	0	0	0
Subject specialist + class teacher	1	5	2	8

Table 7 *The number of schools setting for particular subjects in each year group*

Subject	First year	Second year	Third year	Fourth year
English	5	11	25	29
Science	1	2	8	13
Mathematics	19	31	40	42
French	1	3	26	33

4 The schools' contribution to children's social and personal education

4.1 The schools recognised their responsibility for fostering not only the intellectual development of children but also their wider social and personal development. Some of the experiences contributing to social and personal education were provided directly through the schools' formal curriculum but many more arose from the participation of pupils in the general life of the schools. Day-to-day experiences offered many opportunities for significant informal or incidental learning.

4.2 In almost all the schools visited, children's behaviour was judged to be good or very good. The general picture which emerged from the survey was of relaxed and orderly communities in which teachers were friendly and consistent in their dealings with pupils and where children responded with friendliness and respect towards their fellow pupils, members of staff and other adults. Assemblies, in particular, were making a valuable contribution to the community life of many of the schools.[1] Considerate behaviour was shown in everyday occurrences : children patiently taking turns in physical education, sensibly sharing science apparatus, helping less confident class members in practical subjects, or helping physically handicapped members of the school. In their dealings with teachers and visitors, pupils were generally communicative, helpful and courteous. Although, on occasion, children were seen to be inattentive or to misbehave, such occurrences were infrequent and usually reflected the shortcomings of particular teaching or the personal problems of particular children rather than general inadequacies in the schools. In most schools, a settled atmosphere was established in which pupils worked conscientiously.

4.3 As part of their social and personal education, children need to have a variety of opportunities for cooperation, responsibility, choice and initiative.

---

[1] Paragraph 7.185

In the schools visited they cooperated willingly in activities provided by the teachers as part of the formal curriculum ; their degree of involvement was particularly high in practical subjects such as arts and crafts, physical education and home studies. This spirit of cooperation and involvement was even more marked in out-of-school activities which included games and clubs. Teachers confirmed that this was generally the case when children went on field trips or made contacts with the local community in various activities.

4.4 There was a general expectation in the schools that pupils would act responsibly, and the children's positive response was illustrated by the way they used the schools' shared facilities, their observation of safety procedures, the handling of equipment and the degree to which they were able to work independently. Older pupils, particularly, were allowed to assume a degree of responsibility not just for their own conduct but for some aspects of school life. They acted as librarians, planned and carried out school assemblies, led small groups in exploratory or inquiry work, helped to run clubs and houses, looked after school tuck shops and, in a few schools, undertook duties as prefects. Children generally responded very positively to such opportunities when they arose.

4.5 The exercise of choice by pupils was demonstrated most clearly in out-of-school activities but limited opportunities were also provided within the curriculum where, in some cases, children were able to select appropriate materials and tools for the task in hand or to choose one from a number of possible activities. Choice and responsibility were normally exercised within well-defined limits ; greater possibilities for the exercise of both could be offered in most schools.

4.6 In general, children were not encouraged to show much initiative except in clubs and sporting activities. Within the curriculum, pupils were only rarely expected to initiate new lines of enquiry or to suggest ways of tackling genuinely open-ended problems. In one school, older pupils suggested making a film, which they shot and scripted with the help of a teacher. In another, as part of work in geography related to a local shopping centre, third and fourth year children were encouraged to decide on their own lines of enquiry and to choose ways to present their findings. The quality of children's response to opportunities such as these indicated that schools could profitably extend the range of such opportunities.

4.7 A marked feature of schools in the survey was the provision of voluntary activities which made a major contribution to children's social and personal education. In the schools visited, opportunities out-of-school hours usually included a varied range of sporting activities, outdoor pursuits such as camping and youth hostelling, clubs related to hobbies, and general practical and artistic activities which extended interests developed within the formal curriculum. Activities took place at break times, lunch hours and before and after school ; use was made of school premises and grounds and also local education authority field centres, youth hostels and facilities abroad. Many teachers devoted a considerable amount of their own time to such activities, as did large numbers of children. Such work helped foster closer understanding between teachers and pupils and amongst pupils themselves, and made an important contribution to the settled, caring atmosphere which characterised so many of the schools.

4.8 The quality of pastoral care was another factor which contributed to the well-being of individuals and the general atmosphere of the schools. Pastoral care was judged to good or very good in 36 of the schools and fair in another 10. Children turned to teachers with their personal problems, whether these arose from home circumstances, peer-group pressures, school work or changes associated with puberty. Good pastoral care was found in schools of varying sizes and in schools in a wide variety of settings, varying from affluent neighbourhoods to areas of considerable social disadvantage.

4.9 Schools varied in the extent to which they had explicitly formulated policies for pastoral care. In most schools the policy was implicit ; heads and other senior staff gave a lead by example. The first point of reference was usually the class teacher or form tutor, and when problems arose they were referred to senior staff who had oversight of children's welfare. Heads, and often deputies, were involved in tackling the most serious problems and many made themselves readily available both to children and to parents of children experiencing difficulties. In the most successful schools, heads provided positive and consistent support for children and staff alike. Issues related to pastoral care were often discussed at meetings of year group teachers or at meetings of the whole staff. In many schools good pastoral care was assisted by the close identity younger pupils had with their own class teacher. Schools with good pastoral care ensured that older children did not lose this personal identification with a member of staff even though they were taught by a number of different teachers.

4.10 All the schools in the sample made arrangements to consult with parents about children's progress and their difficulties, through parents' evenings, open days, written reports and individually arranged interviews. In the large majority of schools, contact was made with parents both when pupils were admitted and when they were about to transfer to upper schools. In addition, parents were consulted when major decisions were made about the placement or treatment of children with special needs. About half the schools held meetings with parents to discuss curricular issues and teaching approaches. Home-visiting was not common but was undertaken in a few schools, sometimes by senior staff or, in two cases, by home-liaison teachers. In some cases, very effective work was done by educational welfare officers.

4.11 In about three-quarters of the schools, there was some parental participation in day-to-day work, often in aspects such as home studies, physical education, school journeys or library work. Such participation provided opportunities for parents to identify more closely with the school and for children to work alongside adults other than teachers.

4.12 Over three-quarters of the schools engaged in activities involving the local community. In many cases, music and plays were performed for community audiences. The elderly were entertained and efforts made to collect money for local and national charities. Where localities were well established and relatively compact or where schools provided for a specific religious community, the relations between schools, parents and communities were more readily established. Valuable links between schools, parents and the local community were found in schools serving widely differing communities including localities which had been designated as social priority areas.

5 Provision for children with special educational needs

5.1 The Warnock Report, *Special educational needs* (HMSO 1978), and the Education Act 1981 both drew attention to those children in special and ordinary schools who have special educational needs. The nature of these needs makes varying demands on the resources of the schools. Children may need a modified curriculum, they may need specialised teaching techniques, or they may require special means of access to the curriculum through, for example, special equipment. The survey looked particularly at provision in the middle schools for children with impaired hearing, those with learning difficulties or physical handicaps, and those who had emotional or behavioural problems.

5.2 The identification of children with special educational needs was usually carried out in the first school or, less often, soon after entry to middle schools. In the middle schools, children's progress was assessed informally by teachers as a result of day-to-day contacts and more formally by the use of standardised tests. Assessments were entered on school or local education authority records, along with personal and medical details, where these were relevant. Some records did not provide a broad enough appraisal of children's achievements and difficulties ; there was a tendency for entries to concentrate on fairly narrow areas such as reading. Records were transferred as children moved from one year group to another and from school to school. Sometimes written information in records was supplemented by discussion among the teachers involved.

5.3 Schools made some provision for the needs of those identified as having learning difficulties, where the need was apparent. The most common practice was to withdraw children for additional tuition in reading, writing and number work. Special teaching was also given to children in the lowest sets and streams, and, in six schools, in classes designated as remedial.

Two-thirds of the schools employing withdrawal groups or remedial classes provided appropriate work for children with learning difficulties. About two-thirds of the schools in the survey employed teachers who had special responsibilities for children having learning difficulties ; many of these teachers spent over half their week on such work. Most schools had a variety of apparatus and a wide range of appropriate reading materials but resources for mathematics were not as plentiful as those for reading and other aspects of English. Schemes or guidelines for the work of children with learning difficulties were found in about half the schools but few discussed progression or referred to subjects other than mathematics and English. The work done in withdrawal groups was built on and extended in a number of schools, including one where close liaison with other teachers was maintained by the remedial department. In this school relevant resources were carefully and efficiently used, children's progress was followed through day-to-day observation and the use of objective tests, and good liaison had been established with the schools from which, and to which, pupils transferred.

5.4 In some schools the care and concern shown for pupils were not accompanied by sufficiently expert teaching to enable them to progress appropriately. Not enough attention was devoted to helping older pupils with learning difficulties to cope with the demands of normal class work. Too often, the work offered to these children concentrated too narrowly on reading practice, grammatical and comprehension exercises in English and computational practice in mathematics at the expense of valuable, enriching experiences which were enjoyed by their fellow pupils during the time they were withdrawn. While progress in basic skills is important, the children should also have adequate opportunities to work in other areas such as art, drama and humanities.

5.5 Twelve schools had children assessed as having moderate mental handicap ; most of these pupils were awaiting placement in special schools. In some schools, they were withdrawn from ordinary lessons, and in some they were taught with other children in remedial groups. Some of the schools did not have the resources or skill to provide appropriately for the needs of these children while they were awaiting placement.

5.6 About a quarter of the schools identified a small group of children who had emotional or behavioural difficulties. Consultation with parents, attendance at child guidance centres, visits by educational psychologists and withdrawal for extra help were each used by a number of schools to help meet the needs of such children. Effective ways of catering for such pupils were found in schools where responsibility for these children was seen to lie with the whole staff and where senior staff were able to provide individual counselling. The settled atmosphere and sense of personal concern characteristic of most of the middle schools helped teachers, and the pupils themselves to cope with the latters' emotional or behavioural problems. In general, the special needs of these pupils were being met and they were able to participate in the normal life and work of the school.

5.7 Children with impaired hearing were found in about a quarter of the schools, including two which had special units catering for these pupils. In some schools, children were taught separately by their own teachers and in others, individuals were provided with help for some of the time by specialist teachers of the hearing impaired. There was evidence of close liaison between specialist teachers and class teachers to enable children with impaired hearing to take part in normal lessons as far as possible. Children were regularly tested by specialist teachers in some of the schools but in others there was no systematic policy. In the majority of schools visiting staff supplied equipment to supplement resources found in ordinary classrooms. Overall, schools were giving satisfactory support to these children and enabling them to make satisfactory progress in their work.

5.8 Increasingly, children with physical handicaps are being taught in ordinary classes, either with or without additional personnel or resources, depending on the type and degree of handicap. Children with physical handicaps were taught in fourteen of the schools. In one school a full-time nurse was employed to assist a child with spinal injuries ; in another, extra ancillary help was provided during physical education lessons, and in a third, a peripatetic teacher taught a child for half a day each week. Teachers were aware of some of the difficulties facing physically handicapped children and were attempting to integrate the children into the life and work of the schools.

5.9 Children with physical or sensory handicaps and those with emotional or behavioural difficulties may span the full range of intellectual abilities. In general, teachers were able to help these children so that they were able to participate, as far as possible, in the everyday life of the schools. Schools were less successful in ensuring that the children were challenged with appropriate intellectual demands. Teachers' efforts to meet the special needs of these children would be aided by more specialist advice and support being made available to the schools.

6 The curriculum : planning, assessment and liaison

PLANNING

6.1 The schools were aware of the importance of overall curriculum planning, if children were to develop skills and understandings in each area of the curriculum from the first to the fourth year. Where planning was effective, it helped ensure a reasonable consistency of approach and continuity of experience, and it provided a basis on which decisions could be made about the deployment of staff and the allocation of resources.

6.2 While the heads retained general responsibility for the planning and coordination of the school curriculum they usually delegated responsibility for the planning of the work in specific subjects to other teachers, except where the heads themselves took on particular subject responsibilities. Teachers holding special curricular responsibilities usually drew up schemes of work, sometimes in collaboration with the head and other teachers, and occasionally with local education authority advisers.

6.3 Each of the schools had schemes of work for all or most subjects,[1] though the schemes varied widely in range, comprehensiveness and value. They ranged from those which provided little more than general statements of aims or lists of topics to be taught, to those which gave detailed guidance on aims, content, resources, teaching methods and organisation. Most of the schemes discussed the content to be covered in each year group, but fewer drew attention to the skills, processes and general ideas children were to learn as they progressed through the school.[2] The schemes which identified these skills and processes, suggested appropriate presentation of material and listed available resources were most useful to teachers planning their work. In

---

[1] Table 8 shows the number of schools with schemes of work for particular subjects.
[2] Schemes of work in specific subjects are discussed in Chapter 7.

such cases, the material actually taught was often selected in the light of the schemes and was related to the particular strengths of staff, the availability of resources, and the opportunities provided by the environment of the individual schools.

6.4 Schemes need to be treated as working documents which guide the work of the schools but which are reappraised from time to time to allow for the modification of existing policies and the introduction of new material. In very few of the schools were there arrangements for the systematic reappraisal of schemes of work. Teachers with special curricular responsibilities should have time to consult with other teachers ; to review the documents ; and to appraise the quality and appropriateness of the work done by the children. In reviewing their schemes or devising completely new ones, they might look for guidance to advisers, teachers in other schools and tutors in institutes of higher education, and from materials such as local education authority guidelines, commercially produced resources, and publications from national agencies such as subject associations or the Department of Education and Science. If other members of staff are involved in the process of review, the revised documents are more likely to command general assent and to be used in the day-to-day planning of the work.

ASSESSMENT AND RECORD-KEEPING

6.5 Within the schools assessment took a variety of forms, varying from incidental day-to-day observations of children's progress to formal procedures such as standardised testing or examinations. Assessment helped teachers to gauge children's levels of achievement and to monitor their progress through agreed schemes of work or courses, but was used less often to diagnose children's difficulties or to judge the appropriateness of the work provided for them.

6.6 The schools gave particular attention to assessing children's performance in English. Most operated their own arrangements for the assessment of literacy, though some were involved in local education authority schemes for assessment, usually in addition to their own procedures. About three-quarters of the schools in the sample used some form of standardised testing, usually for children in all year groups. Most often children's attainments in English and mathematics were tested but in some schools tests of reasoning were used. Except in their first year, children of average and above average ability were usually tested once a year, but in almost half the schools using tests, less able children were assessed more frequently. The results of standardised tests were used to record children's progress, to place pupils in streams, bands or sets, and to identify those with specific learning problems. Generally, when pupils were grouped, test results were considered alongside teachers' comments based on observations of children's performance in English. Most schools kept records of children's progress in English through a combination of tests and written assessments by individual teachers. Nearly all schools recorded pupils' achievements on reading schemes but only a few maintained records of pupils' personal reading. In addition to testing, teachers kept account of children's progress by marking their written work, but only a few schools had developed marking policies which helped to ensure comparability of standards. Often, the assessment of children's written work tended to concentrate on the accuracy of spelling and grammar rather than on other important criteria such as the ideas expressed, the range of vocabulary used or the clarity of communication achieved.

6.7 In mathematics, most schools had their own procedures for monitoring pupils' progress through the course, though some schools were involved in local education authority schemes for the assessment of numeracy. About half the schools in the sample used standardised tests in mathematics such as those produced by the National Foundation for Educational Research. In most of these, tests were administered once a year to all pupils and the results used to group pupils for teaching purposes and to record their attainments. There were annual mathematics examinations or tests in the majority of the schools. Few teachers used assessment procedures to diagnose pupils' difficulties or plan appropriate work. Most marking was exclusively concerned with whether answers were right or wrong ; in only a few classes were the methods used to reach answers given sufficient attention when work was marked.

6.8 In 10 schools, teachers assessed pupils' performance in French by using either the En Avant tests or others devised by local education authorities. In many cases children's written work only was graded ; more could be done to assess children's oral competence. Regular written examinations were reported in about a quarter of the schools.

6.9 In craft, design and technology, half the schools kept records of children's work, usually in the form of numerical or letter grades. Pupils' performance was assessed in relation to general criteria such as effort, imaginative ability, perseverance and manual skill. A similar range of criteria were applied to children's work in art, though some teachers found the

41

identification and application of criteria difficult. In only a few schools were children given adequate opportunities to evaluate their own work and that of others. A good example of the relationship between schemes of work, assessment and records was found in one school where the teacher with special responsibility for art made a forecast of the term's work broken down into half-termly and weekly units. Individual pupils' progress and problems were recorded, grades were given on a four-point scale for attitude, effort and attainment, and particular qualities becoming evident in pupils' work were noted.

6.10 Three-quarters of the schools kept records of children's achievement in music, often in the form of marks for writing down patterns of notes, creating simple musical compositions or writing about recorded music. In only a small number of cases were records effective for diagnostic purposes, or were published tests used to help in the selection of children who might benefit from instrumental tuition.

6.11 Records of pupils' achievement in physical education were kept in about three-quarters of the schools. The content of such records included one or more of the following : information about medical problems ; attendance and participation in school teams ; achievements in award schemes ; and comments about performance, attitude, behaviour and dress.

6.12 In other areas of the curriculum such as science, home studies, history and geography, teachers usually awarded marks or grades for individual pieces of work and often administered tests at the completion of work on a particular topic or at the end of a term or school year. Records of children's performance in these areas were rarely detailed but were kept in the majority of schools.

6.13 Numerical scores or grades, sometimes supplemented by comments based on day-to-day observation of children, were normally entered in mark books which teachers consulted when they wrote reports for parents or completed record cards. All but four of the schools had their own internal records which were transferred as children moved through the school. Standardised test results were passed on from year group to year group in 42 schools and samples of children's work in just over half the schools. Twenty-eight of the schools made some use of local authority records to transfer information about children's achievements from one year group to the next.

6.14 In general, the schools need to reappraise their policies for assessment and record-keeping so that they play a more positive role in developing the work. As well as providing information about children's achievements and progress, assessment can be used as a way of diagnosing pupils' difficulties and of helping teachers appraise the extent to which the work done is suitable for children's varying abilities. It can also foster self-evaluation by involving children in the assessment of their own work and that of others.

6.15 As part of their reappraisal, the schools might consider whether too much or too little emphasis is being given to the assessment of work and the completion of records in specific areas of the curriculum. In order to foster comparability of standards and expectations, the criteria used to assess children's work need to be made explicit. Decisions should be taken as to whether the range of criteria needs to be widened to include previously unassessed aspects of the work and as to how far criteria apply across the curriculum or only to specific subjects within it. In particular, the schools might consider devising policies for marking which are agreed and implemented by all teaching staff. Marking needs to be seen as a constructive activity concerned less with identifying and correcting particular errors and more with assessing children's levels of under-standing, discovering the causes of their mistakes and suggesting possible remedies. To achieve this, marking may have to be done more intensively and more selectively.

CONTINUITY AND LIAISON

6.16 The schools were making considerable efforts to pass on information about pupils and to consult with colleagues about the curriculum in an attempt to achieve greater continuity of experience for children as they moved from first to middle to upper school. Factors which influenced arrangements made for continuity and liaison included the time heads and teachers were able to give, and the importance they attached, to the task ; the support given by local education authority advisers and administrators ; the distance between schools and, in particular, the number of schools involved. The greater the number of first and upper schools with which they had to consult, the more difficult it was for the middle schools to establish reasonable continuity. As Tables 9 and 10 show, 28 of the schools in the survey each received children from more than five first schools ; and 21 of the schools each sent pupils to four or more upper schools.

Liaison with first schools

6.17 Various means were used to ease children's transition from the first to the middle schools. In all the middle schools except one, introductory visits were arranged for children from first schools. In many cases, middle school teachers responsible for coordinating the work of first year classes visited children in their first schools. Almost all the first schools completed and passed on local education authority record cards ; many supplemented these with their own records. The results of standardised tests were passed on to two-thirds of the middle schools and samples of children's work to almost half. About two-thirds of the middle schools reported that they provided some information to first schools on children's subsequent progress.

6.18 There were many examples of effective liaison between first and middle schools to provide continuity of provision for children with special needs, especially for slow learners. Often, information from records was supplemented by that gained from inter-school visiting where pupils could be observed at work and their needs discussed with their class teachers.

6.19 Table 11 shows the number of middle schools whose head reported that the staff consulted with first school teachers about the curriculum. Most middle schools consulted with first schools over work in mathematics, sometimes as a result of working parties convened by local education authority advisers. Although a third of the schools made little or no use of information from their first schools, many middle schools used knowledge of children's previous progress in mathematics to place them in ability groups, to identify those in need of additional help, and, sometimes, to determine the point at which children started on mathematics schemes. About three-quarters of the schools consulted with first schools about children's progress in the skills of reading. The information transferred usually included reading ages and comments on individuals needing remedial help. Where liaison was good, the reading schemes and handwriting practices of the first schools were continued in the middle schools and information about pupils' subsequent progress was sent back. In about a fifth of the schools, teachers met with colleagues from first schools to plan music festivals and, in a few cases, peripatetic teachers provided continuity of instrumental tuition for children transferring from first schools. In general, however, not many of the middle schools consulted with their contributory schools to foster continuity of work in subjects other than mathematics and English. The schools need to consider liaison with first schools in other respects than language and number and whether appropriate use is being made of information received from their contributory schools.

Liaison with other middle schools

6.20 In general, teachers were willing to consult with colleagues in other middle schools in an attempt to reach agreement about the content of the work to be taught, but good intentions did not always result in effective coordination of policies and practice. In many of the survey schools, the heads reported that their staff met with colleagues from other middle schools to discuss the curriculum, especially French, mathematics, science and English (see Table 12). In a number of local education authorities, advisers had set up working parties to draw up guidelines on the teaching of specific subjects. Some good examples of inter-school cooperation were reported, but in general, greater attention needs to be given to coordinating the work of the middle schools in a locality to achieve more consistent coverage of important aspects of the curriculum.

Liaison with upper schools

6.21 Most of the schools were aware of the importance of continuity with upper schools. Almost all the middle schools reported that their pupils made introductory visits to upper schools. In some cases, teachers from upper schools visited middle schools to talk to pupils prior to transfer ; exceptionally, upper school teachers had regular teaching commitments in the middle schools. Over three-quarters of the schools reported passing on pupils' records to upper schools, particularly records for English, French, mathematics and science. A similar proportion passed on the results of standardized tests, and just over half reported sending on samples of work of individual pupils. Sixty teachers in the sample had particular responsibility for liaison with upper schools ; many of these were fourth year coordinators, though some were teachers with special curricular responsiblities.

6.22 As Table 13 shows, the heads of over four-fifths of the middle schools reported consultations with all or some of their upper schools in relation to mathematics, French, science and English. Half the schools in the sample used the same set of mathematics texts as their upper schools ; in a rather higher proportion, the content of their mathematics curriculum had been influenced by upper schools. There were twelve examples of effective liaison in physical education, and there were a small number of cases where upper schools had directly influenced what was taught in geography. Only in a few schools were schemes of work exchanged with upper schools. Further development of the exchange of schemes between upper and middle schools could provide background information leading to more effective continuity between the phases of education. In some areas, regular meetings between teachers from upper schools and all contributory middle schools had been established by local education authority advisers in an attempt to achieve greater continuity. In one, teachers of French had reached agreement on expectations of pupils' progress, the transfer of records and examination arrangements ; in another, teachers of physical education from contributory middle schools had met with staff from the upper schools to reach agreement about programmes of work, competitions and the provision of kit. There was a number of good examples of liaison involving inter-school visiting and discussion of pupils with special needs.

6.23 It is particularly important that effective curricular liaison should be established with upper schools so that on transfer pupils are not held back and made to cover the same ground. For continuity of experience to be secured, both the middle and the upper schools need to work closely together, exchanging information about pupils and dove-tailing, as far as possible, their approaches to the curriculum. Curriculum continuity is hard to achieve even when circumstances are favourable, but it is especially difficult where a system of parental choice operates so that at thirteen children transfer to a large number of upper schools.

ANNEX TO CHAPTER 6

Table 8   The number of schools with schemes of work for particular subjects

Subject	Number of schools with schemes of work
English	46
Art and design	46
Craft, design and technology	38
Religious education	41
History	47
Geography	47
Science	45
Mathematics	47
Music	45
Physical education	45
French	43
Home studies	46
Needlecrafts	42

Table 9   The number of middle schools receiving children from various numbers of first schools – by size of middle school

Number of first schools from which children transferred	'Small' middle schools	'Medium-sized' middle schools	'Large' middle schools	All middle schools
1–2	4	4	0	8
3–5	4	4	4	12
6–10	1	9	6	16
11–15	0	7	3	10
16 +	0	1	1	2

Table 10   The number of middle schools transferring children to various numbers of upper schools – by size of middle school

Number of upper schools to which children transferred	'Small' middle schools	'Medium-sized' middle schools	'Large' middle schools	All middle schools
1	2	2	6	10
2	5	4	1	10
3	1	3	3	7
4	0	3	2	5
5	0	5	0	5
6 +	1	8	2	11

Table 11 The number of middle schools with teachers engaging in consultation with those in first schools – by subject

Subject	Number of schools
Mathematics	38
English	37
Remedial teaching	24
Music	14
Physical education	10
Religious education	9
Science	9
Art and design	8
Environmental studies	7
Humanities	5
History	3
Geography	3
Craft, design and technology	2
English as a second language	2
Social studies	2
French	1
Multi-racial education	1
Needlecrafts	1
Other modern foreign languages	1
Home studies	0
Rural studies	0

Table 12 The number of middle schools with teachers engaging in consultation with those in other middle schools – by subject

Subject	Number of schools
French	42
Mathematics	39
Science	38
English	37
Physical education	31
Craft, design and technology	27
Music	27
Art and design	25
Home studies	25
Religious education	25
Geography	24
Remedial teaching	24
History	21
Needlecrafts	17
Humanities	12
Social studies	8
Environmental studies	7
Multi-racial education	3
English as a second language	2
Rural studies	2
Other modern foreign languages	1

Table 13   The number of middle schools with teachers engaging in consultation with those in upper schools – by subject

Subject	Number of schools
Mathematics	47
French	46
Science	44
English	41
Remedial teaching	36
Geography	29
Music	29
Physical education	29
Art and design	27
Religious education	27
Craft, design and technology	26
History	26
Home studies	26
Needlecrafts	20
Humanities	13
Health education	8
Social studies	8
Environmental studies	6
Other modern foreign languages	6
English as a second language	2
Multi-racial education	2
Rural studies	2

7 The content of the curriculum

7.1 This chapter begins by considering the contribution the schools were making to the development of children's ability to use and respond to language, not just in English lessons but in all areas of the curriculum. Subsequent sections deal with particular subjects, though it should be recognised that not every school in the survey used these precise subject divisions in constructing their timetables or in planning their work.

7.2 The sections contain a number of overall assessments of standards achieved, based on observations of work seen. During the inspections, specific assessments of work were made in particular subjects but in addition more general areas such as personal and social education or language and literacy were judged. To make assessments of the work related to specific subjects, account was taken not only of activities in lessons timetabled specifically for the subjects but also of work observed elsewhere in the curriculum, which contributed to children's understanding of the subjects, for example, the contribution of mathematics to practical subjects. Following the inspections, overall assessments were made of the general standards of work achieved in each subject in each school. In addition, for each subject the appropriateness of the work was assessed throughout the age range for (a) the large proportion of children in the middle range of ability in each school, (b) the minority of children of above average ability in each school, and (c) the minority of children of below average ability in each school. It should be remembered that underlying the generalisations provided in relation to each subject there were considerable variations in the standards achieved by different groups of children within the same school as well as in different schools.

LANGUAGE AND LITERACY

7.3 Opportunities for language development occurred in all areas of the curriculum through the four modes of reading, writing, talking and listening. All the schools made formal provision for English on the timetable. The development of children's ability to read and write was a major priority, though in many of the schools more could have been done to extend children's skills so that they could use the written word in different ways for different purposes.

7.4 The first part of this section discusses the organisation and planning of the work in English and describes those activities such as spelling, punctuation and poetry, the teaching of which was largely confined to timetabled English lessons. The second part examines activities such as reading and writing which were important components of English lessons but also given substantial attention in many other areas of the curriculum.

English

7.5 English was almost always taught as a separate subject though in a few schools it formed part of humanities programmes for some year groups. On average, the schools devoted just over a fifth of their time to the subject for the younger year groups ; this proportion fell slightly in the third and fourth years. Two-thirds of all teachers in the schools taught some English. The older the children the more likely they were to be taught the subject by teachers who taught English for a considerable proportion of the week and who had studied it during initial training. In just over two-thirds of the schools first and second year pupils were taught English in mixed-ability classes. In over half the sample, third and fourth year pupils had English in classes formed according to ability. Many schools used setting in the subject as a way of providing for different abilities, including the most able. Just over two-thirds of the schools withdrew some children from their classes for extra help with reading and writing, most frequently in the first two years. Six schools formed classes which they designated as remedial and in which English formed a substantial proportion of the programme of work.

7.6 Almost all the schools had schemes of work for English as a separate subject. Many schemes gave considerable attention to grammar, punctuation, spelling and handwriting. A few provided book lists to assist teachers to choose novels, poems and course books appropriate to particular age groups or levels of ability. Details of audio-visual equipment and materials were sometimes given, but there were few references to methods of teaching to be employed or to progression in the learning of skills. Only a few schemes dealt in sufficient depth with the means of extending reading, the diagnosis of individuals' problems, and the monitoring of pupils' progress. Too often, schemes did not have any major influence on day-to-day work.

7.7 Comprehension, grammar, and spelling formed a considerable part of the English curriculum in most of the sample. English course books were used in almost every school. Some of these introduced children to well-written poetry and excerpts of prose from established writers, but many course books concentrated on less valuable comprehension and grammatical exercises. In many schools, particularly but not exclusively in the first two years, there was undue reliance on course books and work sheet exercises, often unrelated to other language work, a practice which restricted pupils to single-word or single-sentence answers, and which appeared to have little effect on children's ability to understand or to produce written prose. Frequently, the extended prose written by able children showed a competence far exceeding that tested by the grammatical exercises set for them. The teaching and testing of spelling were often based on published lists. Some teachers drew up lists of words which had been frequently mis-spelt and used these for spelling sessions ; others made lists of key words which children needed to use in specific subjects. There were many examples seen of spelling lists which had no relevance to the work children were doing or to their levels of understanding. Work produced for display was often written with great accuracy, especially when provided by older, able pupils. However, despite the time devoted to punctuation and spelling in many schools, some children continued to find these aspects of writing difficult. Pupils were making good progress in those schools which set realistic, written assignments that demanded and developed accuracy in punctuation and spelling. Schools were rightly concerned that children should be competent in these aspects of the work but many needed to review the balance of activities they provided, especially the emphasis often placed on text-book exercises which were not closely related to the everyday use of written language.

7.8 The reading and writing of poetry were largely confined to timetabled English lessons, though in a few schools poems such as modern versions of *Beowulf* or *The Canterbury Tales* were used in drama lessons or linked to work in humanities. Although children had opportunities to hear verse in just over half the sample, poetry appeared to be a low priority in most of the schools. The provision of poetry books was good in only 9 of the sample, but satisfactory in a further 17. Where appropriate poetry by writers such as

Hughes, Stephens or Farjeon was read aloud in class, the great majority of children appeared to enjoy the experience. Where children were allowed a choice of what to read, some chose to read poetry, frequently from anthologies of comic verse. Children's enjoyment of poetry was enhanced where, in a few cases, schools had invited in poets to read and talk about their work. Frequently, however, poetry was used by teachers only as source material for comprehension exercises and for handwriting practice ; for some children their only contact with poetry was through course books. In the majority of the schools, pupils were expected to be able to write verse. Many tackled this writing enthusiastically and with some success. In a few schools, children wrote poetry based on models such as Belloc's *Cautionary Verses* and Dylan Thomas's *Under Milk Wood* ; many successfully captured the rhythms and stylistic devices of the originals and strengthened their own style at the same time. Much of the best poetry resulted from reflection on personal experience. The following example of work by a fourth year pupil illustrates the care and sensitivity with which some children approached their writing :

Anger is like a piece of paper on fire
It flares up in a flurry of flame
And then dies in a black mass of dust and confusion.

Sometimes anger is like a smouldering autumn bonfire
It creeps into your very being
With its sourness and sting.

7.9 Drama, too, can help children reflect on, and extend, their personal experience, as well as foster their self-confidence and their ability to express their own thoughts and feelings in a variety of contexts. In half of the survey schools, drama was a timetabled activity for some classes, and in a further quarter, it was part of the curriculum, though not formally timetabled. In addition to, or instead of, timetabled drama, productions such as *Joseph and the Technicolour Dreamcoat* and *Charlie and the Chocolate Factory*, were mounted as extra-curricular activities in many schools. Sixteen schools had separate accommodation for drama; this ranged from good to inadequate. In the remaining schools, lack of accommodation for drama was often a constraint. Drama was often linked to preparation for class assemblies and as a result children developed confidence in presenting material to audiences. It was occasionally used in other subject areas as a way of helping children to enter imaginatively into the experience of others, for example, history and environmental studies. The benefits accruing from such opportunities were clearly seen in one school where fourth year children wrote effective dialogue and gained insights into imaginative literature through a dramatic exploration of *Flannan Isle*. Almost always children responded well and enjoyed activities in drama. Some teachers made use of materials from the BBC or from commercial publishers, which often enabled children to link their work in drama with their writing. There was a tendency for teachers with little experience of drama teaching not to venture far beyond games, which, though enjoyed, limited the experience drama could offer children. Similarly, there was often a lack of progression in drama teaching and too little provision for reflection or discussion of insights gained. A few schools had drama clubs in addition to, or independent of, timetabled provision. Groups of children from some schools made visits to local theatres, took part in drama festivals, or watched theatre-in-education groups perform. There was particularly good provision in one school which served a social priority area. The school had three drama clubs, timetabled a one hour session of drama for all children each week, and encouraged pupils to write scripts which were subsequently produced by them in closed-circuit television presentations. Groups from this school had visited the local theatre, and stayed for several days at Stratford-on-Avon and had mounted many annual productions.

Language work in the curriculum as a whole

7.10 Reading, writing, listening, and, to a lesser extent, talking were aspects of language which both teachers of English and of other subjects attempted to foster. Language as communication of what had been learned was stressed at the expense of language as part of the activity of learning itself, though some good examples of language used in the process of learning were observed. Just under a third of the schools had written guidelines on language work across the curriculum ; in a few cases, these had been provided by local education authority advisers. In the remaining schools, individual heads and teachers often influenced practice, but too frequently there was insufficient coordination of language work.

7.11 Talking is a major means of making sense of experience and communicating with others. Through appropriate teaching, children can acquire a wide range of language uses so that they can speak appropriately in different contexts, including those where standard forms of speech are required. Only a small number of the schools in the survey regularly provided opportunities for children to discuss themes or issues, either in small groups or as a class. Where effective use of children's talk occurred, it was usually associated with good teacher-pupil relationships. In such classes, children were able to contribute their own ideas, questions and accounts of experiences in the expectation that these would be thoughtfully considered by their teachers and fellow pupils. Many teachers took care to explain the meaning of key words in their subjects. In most schools, talk played an important part in practical subjects such as art and home studies, but examples of good practice were also seen in other subject areas : examples of lively dialogues in French, and occasionally in mathematics where puzzles and games encouraged and challenged children's language as they wrestled with problems in cooperation with one another. For much of the time, however, teachers talked and the children listened. A further difficulty, often noted, was that teachers were insufficiently demanding of older children in oral exchanges and tended to treat them as younger than they were, both in the vocabulary used and the extensive use of closed questions which frequently required one-word answers. In those schools where open-ended questions were discussed in small groups or as a class children frequently displayed an ability to adapt their language for different purposes. In general, however, the children in the survey schools need more opportunities to pose questions, put forward arguments, speculate, solve problems, and discuss the work they are doing.

7.12 In the first-year classes, almost all the children could read well enough to comprehend material appropriate to their age and general ability. In three-fifths of the sample there were features of good practice in the teaching of reading ; these included the encouragement of personal reading, systematic monitoring of pupils' progress, class libraries of books appropriate to children's abilities and the provision of readers and supplementary readers often colour-coded according to level of difficulty, and sometimes linked to schemes used in the first schools. Other schools, however, had no structured approach to developing pupils' reading and no effective means of monitoring the progress of children except for those requiring remedial help. One consequence of this was that some children, particularly in years one and two, were found attempting books substantially too difficult for them and becoming discouraged ; conversely, some children were losing their enthusiasm for reading as a result of work which was insufficiently stimulating.

7.13 By the fourth year the majority of children could read adequately for everyday purposes. However, a small minority needed help to cope with the material they were asked to read in class. Judging from the reading records teachers and children kept in some schools, many fourth year pupils read quite extensively and some were adept at using books as sources of information as well as for pleasure. In all schools, it would be useful both for children and teachers if pupils were encouraged to keep their own records of what they read.

7.14 In a small number of schools, reading skills were being systematically extended to enable pupils to approach the printed word in different ways for different purposes. For example, pupils could skim passages rapidly or they could use a variety of techniques to examine passages in detail in order to explore their meaning. In about half the schools, such skills were taught in English lessons but not applied to work being undertaken in other parts of the curriculum. In general, attempts to extend reading skills involved comprehension exercises which did not allow children to consider wider, deeper, issues or to explore relationships between the passages they were examining and other reading. On occasions, project work gave opportunities for children to extract, compare, and sift information from various sources, so developing their powers of discrimination and evaluation. This happened in relatively few instances, usually where children had free access to well-stocked libraries.

7.15 Although English or language guidelines nearly always emphasised the importance of reading for pleasure, the time available for this activity varied considerably from school to school. In about half of the sample, the children were given some time each week specifically for reading, though many often read during registration or in other spare moments. In some schools, teachers guided the reading of individual children, read extracts aloud to stimulate interest, and selected books of good quality for school use. In one such school, there was a reading session of 20 minutes each day in which everyone, including the teachers, read silently. Where such provision for reading was made, the response of the majority of the children was good. One second year girl, for example, had, in four terms, read thirty-three books including Garner's *Elidor*, Adams' *Watership Down* and Williamson's *Tarka the Otter*. This appeared typical of many abler children of this age. Children's attitudes to books were influenced by the teaching staff, by the home, and, often strongly, by the peer group. In one school lists of children's recommendations were displayed and in another, children's interest in books was manifested by an informal network which recommended and circulated novels by Tolkien, Lewis, and a sixty-page novel written on a family theme by one of the children. In many schools, the interest and enthusiasm of the majority of children were not sufficiently matched by opportunities to talk about their individual reading and to receive guidance and recommendations which would develop it. This kind of work should be given greater priority by teachers. In most of the schools, teachers regularly read passages to their pupils, in some cases as an introduction to written work and in other cases mainly for pleasure. Some teachers were too concerned to extract the maximum amount of information from the text they were reading and undervalued the benefits and the pleasure children derived from hearing good material read effectively.

7.16 Links between literature and other areas of the curriculum were made in some schools but not often on a planned basis. There were some examples of books being used to extend children's understanding of different times and places. In one school, *I am David* was linked to a project on The Year of the Child ; in another, an extract from *Hard Times* was related to work on 19th century social history ; in a third, the teacher of a first year class read *Stig of the Dump* to her children as an extension of a project on the Stone Age. The use of fiction to extend children's awareness and understanding could be used more often, and to greater effect, in most of the schools.

7.17 Children were often encouraged to make use of libraries for personal reading. In many schools, new library books were displayed attractively and in some, children had regular library lessons where books could be exchanged and advice sought from teachers on further reading. Attempts were made, not always successfully, to teach children to make effective use of libraries. Many libraries had good features but also limitations, which included restricted borrowing policies, inadequate provision for the full age and ability range, and limited access during the school day. Many of the schools need to review their arrangements for library opening hours and for the borrowing of books so as to make full use of the stocks available. In many of the survey schools, children had been taken to local public libraries in school time and benefited from contacts with children's librarians. This was not possible in rural areas with relatively few library services ; there, pupils were particularly dependent on school libraries. Where these were unsatisfactory, children were particularly disadvantaged.

7.18 In two-thirds of the schools, books were sold through clubs of various kinds, which sometimes operated in addition to school bookshops. Particularly in areas where children did not have ready access to new books outside school, clubs and bookshops were valuable in stimulating children's interest in reading and in acting as focal points where pupils and teachers could share their enthusiasm for books. In some schools, bring-and-buy sales of second-hand books were organised ; and at open evenings in some, parents were able to buy books for their own children and for the school library. In one area, sixth formers from the upper school organised an annual book exchange for the benefit of children in the middle school.

7.19 Children of all ages and abilities devoted a considerable amount of time to the writing of prose. The quality of children's writing was considered to be generally good in 9 schools, and fair in a further 31. The best writing, characterised by directness, clarity and vigour, was usually based on children's first-hand experience of activities such as field-trips or practical investigations and on work where children provided imaginary eye-witness accounts. Similarly, in classroom-based imaginative writing which had been preceded by preparation and discussion, the enjoyment of the task and success of the results were evident. In many schools, children produced much written material, often very carefully presented, but much of this work was copied and not often based on personal understanding accompanied by individual choice of language. In some schools less able children devoted too little time to writing continuous prose and made correspondingly little progress in improving their ability to write stories and accounts.

7.20 In 6 of the schools, preparation for written work was extensive ; it included local visits, school broadcasts, extended discussion, the reading of extracts from novels and poems, or the use of other stimuli such as drama. In some other schools where insufficient material was presented for consideration or where too little time was given to discussion and reflection, children found writing difficult.

7.21 Assistance during writing was usually helpful and encouraging ; teachers tended to spend more time helping the less able than assisting the more able to find the most effective expression of their ideas. Much of the marking was supportive, though the majority of teachers reacted mainly to spelling, presentation and handwriting. Some commented on content, but only a few referred to structure or appropriateness of expression. More attention needs to be paid to these aspects when marking or commenting on children's work.

7.22 Some schools encouraged the children to present their completed work at assemblies, to read their stories to the class, and, occasionally, to write books for local first schools. In general, the children need more opportunities to write for a variety of purposes in a range of styles and to write for real or imagined readers other than teachers.

7.23 In four-fifths of the schools, the presentation of written work was either good or satisfactory ; in some of these, it was very good indeed. Most schools laid considerable stress on the quality of presentation ; in some classes there was over-emphasis on neatness, and children's work was judged more in terms of its tidy appearance than of its content.

7.24 In almost half the schools, teachers had agreed on the styles of handwriting to be taught. In a few, there was a policy which was applied to all age groups, was implemented across the curriculum, and allowed for progression, including the need for increased speed. In such schools, links were often made with first schools and display was often used as a stimulus for good handwriting. Some teachers used a standardised script for all their displays, overhead transparencies and blackboard work. In only a few schools were attempts made to help children having difficulty with handwriting.

7.25 Schools varied considerably in the degree to which they made use of pupils' out-of-school experiences to foster language development. In many schools, little reference was made to television programmes which teachers considered to be beneficial. Posters linking books to particular programmes were displayed in some schools and generated interest among pupils. Few teachers related pupils' personal reading to current work and consequently the possible links were often left to the children themselves. Although schools often acknowledged their role in counteracting negative influences from the locality, there was sometimes a failure to recognise and make use of the strengths of the community such as its folklore or the skills and interests of its members.

7.26 Overall, standards of work were satisfactory or better in two-thirds of the sample including one-sixth where standards were good. In the schools with satisfactory standards children were producing good work in some, though not all, aspects of language. In general, pupils of average ability were better provided for than those of above or below average ability. Although many schools attempted to provide appropriately for children of different abilities through the introduction of setting, both the more able and the less able children were not given enough suitable activities in a majority of the schools.

59

MATHEMATICS

7.27 In all the schools mathematics was taught as a separate subject to all children. On average, the younger pupils spent just under one-fifth of the time on mathematics ; the average proportion was slightly lower for the older children. Such a reduction in time was reasonable, as more time was made available for subjects such as science or craft, design and technology, where mathematics could be applied. Schools varied considerably in the amount of time they allocated to mathematics : in some schools , pupils were given about two-thirds as much time as were pupils of the same age group in others. There was no clear connection between the time allocated to the subject and the quality of the work.

7.28 Mathematics was taught by just over half the total number of teachers in the sample. It was usually taught to classes formed according to ability, except in the first year when pupils were taught in mixed-ability classes in over half the schools. Second, third and fourth year registration groups were, in most cases, reorganised into sets according to children's attainment in mathematics. Setting was regarded by the schools as an appropriate way of providing for the range of their pupils' abilities. In some schools, children who were least able were taught in groups withdrawn from mixed-ability classes.

7.29 The schools attached considerable importance to the processes of addition, subtraction, multiplication and division. Computing involving whole numbers and fractions was practised regularly by children of all abilities. Such regular practice did not always result in the facility with number which was sought, especially when the principles underlying calculations were left obscure or where the calculations were not related to useful problems. Too much time was often spent in the routine practice of skills, particularly by the less able. Pupils were often proficient at the set rules but unable to apply them in unfamiliar situations. The complexity of the work on fractions in many schools was hard to justify when it could not be related to any application. Even when applications were given, they were not always realistic. One examination question, for example, asked for the length of wood remaining when 10 per cent was cut from a piece 350 metres long.

7.30 In almost every school importance was rightly given to decimals, but, as with fractions, considerable emphasis was often placed on computational practice devoid of application, particularly for average and abler pupils. Relatively few opportunities were given to apply decimals in the practical context of shopping, of weighing, of measuring areas and volumes, of using percentages, or of constructing scale drawings. In one school, a class of 10 year olds were working through a long exercise in a text book to find the area of rectangles. Many of the examples were given in an everyday context but the class ignored this to concentrate on the calculation of length times breadth. One question was concerned with finding the area of a concrete path 17 metres long x 0.5 metres wide. The great majority of children wrote down a multiplication sum involving 5 x 17 and the placing of the decimal point. One child, who was having difficulty, attempted to pace out the 17 metre path in the classroom. He noted that this was impossible in the space available, but realised that by halving the length he could consider the path as two adjacent sections of width one metre. By using his commonsense he was able to write down immediately the area as 8.5 sq. metres.

7.31 In over a third of the schools, inadequate attention was given to mental arithmetic and this often resulted in a poor knowledge of number bonds and an undue reliance on standard routines for calculation. In most of the schools, more attention needs to be given to the promotion of mathematical discussion concerned, for example, with the variety of commonsense methods which could be used in calculation, or with the consideration of the accuracy of a variety of methods of measuring weight, area or volume. Mental mathematics and discussion also provide means of developing the skills of estimation and approximation, which were adequately stressed in only a few schools. In very many schools, the practice of computation was so extensive that it prevented the adequate development of other work of a graphical, geometric or logical nature. Children need, in these schools, to be given more encouragement to devise their own methods of calculation through greater emphasis on the practice of mental mathematics.

7.32 Graphical work was a component of mathematics courses, but in some schools, such work lacked progression and not even the most able children had opportunities to proceed beyond the drawing of block graphs. Graphical work was sometimes undertaken in other subject areas, but was not always developed. Many schools conducted traffic surveys, for example, which led to the drawing of graphs but not always to discussion of mathematical ideas such as scale or to the interpretation and explanation of the results displayed. All but four of the schools paid little attention to creative work : pupils were not given enough opportunities to investigate problems, to solve puzzles, or to use their imagination in mathematics. An interesting use of puzzles was seen at one school where the mathematics coordinator had, over a number of years, built up a collection of three-dimensional wooden jig-saws. At the time when he introduced children to work on the volume of solids, he displayed these jig-saws prominently in his classroom. Children from remedial groups were as keen as their more able peers to attempt to dismantle and reassemble the puzzles at break and lunch time. In many more of the schools children need to be given opportunities to appreciate the creative aspects of mathematics.

7.33 Too few of the schools set tasks requiring children to work with a variety of measuring instruments or to study the geometrical aspects of natural and man-made forms. In many cases, children were not encouraged to explore patterns and to discuss the generalisations underlying such patterns. However, some examples of good practice were seen. In one first year mixed-ability class, pairs of children were set the task of finding the area of an irregular template. Pairs of abler children drew around the template on paper marked off in square centimetres, and less able children used paper marked off in squares each with an area of four square centimetres. When the data had been collected, the relationship between the numbers in the fifties provided by the less able pupils and those in the two-hundreds provided by the abler children was found to derive from the number of small squares which fitted into the larger ones. The most able children were given the further task of making different shapes with twelve squares. After working with materials and after considerable discussion, the children obtained, in their own language, the conclusions that "Although the shapes all contain the same number of squares inside, they have different perimeters" and "The perimeter is smaller when they have fewer outside pieces". A second example where the pupils were encouraged to discuss patterns and make generalisations occurred in work on Pascal's Triangle. The teacher introduced the subject to able fourth year pupils through discussing a traffic scheme which involved heavy goods lorries crossing three Tyne Bridges in the ratio of 1:2:1. The pupils were then set the task of extending the scheme to other situations where four, five or more bridges were to be used.

7.34 Except in some aspects of computation, there was considerable variation among the schools in the range of topics included in their courses and in the proportion of their pupils to whom these topics were taught. For example, among the topics traditionally included in mathematics syllabuses, areas of circles, volumes of prisms and angle properties of polygons were studied by almost all fourth year pupils in some schools and by none in others. Early work on negative numbers and simple linear equations was given to almost all the oldest pupils in some schools and to less than half in others. The same variation was noted for topics more recently introduced into school syllabuses, such as operations on sets, number bases, probability and geometrical transformations. Familiarity with the language of sets can have a unifying influence on the development of much of school mathematics ;

work in different number bases can be used to develop understanding of many familiar computational techniques ; and simple ideas of both probability and geometrical transformations give children many opportunities to develop logical and spatial concepts through practical activities. Efforts made to promote liaison and continuity with other middle schools in the locality need to be strengthened to provide a more consistent coverage of important aspects of the mathematics curriculum. Such consultation may lead to agreement on the scope and depth of treatment to be given to important mathematical topics in the middle schools of an area.

7.35 Practical activity was regarded as an important aspect of mathematics in only half the schools, and then, in some cases, by only a minority of the teachers. Practical activities, often suggested in text books, were frequently omitted or curtailed, especially in the work of the older pupils. In about two-thirds of the schools, the provision of apparatus was satisfactory, but even where there was a good range of apparatus and of materials such as maps or timetables, too little use was made of them. The use of resources was sometimes further restricted by their limited accessibility and by teachers' lack of knowledge of what was available in the schools. In the great majority of schools, teachers need greater guidance when to use the equipment available to help children to understand mathematics.

7.36 Few schools included investigational work on the local environment, though the potential contribution of such work to children's knowledge of mathematics was considerable. School buildings and grounds were sometimes used for measuring, estimating, scale drawing and elementary surveying. Other activities included surveys of shopping habits and comparisons of supermarket prices. Field-work in other subjects such as geography made a contribution to mathematics in some schools ; in one, the teacher with designated responsibility for mathematics attended field trips to advise on statistical work. To encourage pupils to apply mathematics to everyday situations, teachers in a few schools made good use of resources such as train timetables and home extension plans.

7.37 In most of the schools, textbooks and workcards provided illustrations of how mathematics could be applied but children rarely had opportunities to apply their mathematical knowledge and skills to problems arising out of experience. These were applied to some extent in other subject areas, but rarely was their application planned as part of an overall mathematics policy. Graphical representation was seen, for example, in science, geography and topic work ; weighing and measuring in home studies and science ; symmetry and tesselations in art and needlecrafts. In one class, a teacher revised the idea of proportion when discussing the ratio of sand to cement for concrete mixing. In another, work on crystals in science was linked to the geometry of solids in mathematics. In general, however, much encouragement is needed for children to apply the mathematics they have learned to other subjects and to everyday situations.

7.38 In the majority of lessons observed, teaching was directed at the whole class, after which children worked individually through the material that had been set. Such work was sometimes differentiated according to pupils' abilities. More individual work was done in some schools by the younger pupils or by those who were less able at mathematics. In 5 schools, children in all four year groups had individual programmes of work. In a large majority of the schools, the work was heavily teacher-directed, with few opportunities for pupils to exercise initiative. However, pupils in a few schools were allowed to use a variety of methods or to exercise some choice of, for example, workcards, reference books or games and puzzles.

7.39 All the schools set homework in mathematics for at least some of their pupils. It was set more commonly for older pupils than younger ones but in about a quarter of the schools, it was given to pupils of all ages and abilities. Most homework tasks required pupils to complete exercises started in class.

7.40 A good feature in many schools was the care children took in the presentation of written work in their books. In about a third of the sample, children's work in mathematics was displayed satisfactorily in specialist rooms or in other parts of the school, but in many schools, more effective use could have been made of display to motivate children and to contribute to the teaching and learning of mathematics.

7.41 Almost every school had a scheme of work for mathematics as a separate subject. The exceptions were one school where the scheme contained combined as well as separate sections for mathematics and science, and one where there was no scheme. Nearly half of the local education authorities had produced guidelines for mathematics in middle schools ; the influence of these guidelines was most marked in those schools where teachers with special responsibility for mathematics had served on the working parties. In two cases, common syllabuses had been agreed with other middle schools in the locality. Most schemes concentrated on listing the topics to be covered. These lists were of limited use unless they spelt out the emphasis to be given each topic, and the depth and breadth of treatment required. Stages of progression were sometimes indicated by discussing how topics could be developed from year to year, and in a small number of schemes the content to be covered by children of average ability in each year group was carefully specified. The development of one such topic is illustrated below:

Topic – angles

Year 1

a. vocabulary of lines – vertical, horizontal, oblique, diagonal, perpendicular

b. right angles – where vertical and horizontal meet eg in the classroom

c. making right angles – geo-strips, cardboard, etc.

d. comparing angles with right angles, acute, obtuse, reflex

e. moving clockwise, anticlockwise through right angles (complete turn – 360°, right angle – 90°)

f. N S E W – turning to face directions, half turn, full turn

g. half a right angle – 45° – 8 compass points

h. estimation of size of angles

Year 2

a. revision of vocabulary

b. interior angles of a triangle, square, rectangle. Angles on a straight line

c. extension to find angle sum of a triangle – using cut outs

d. use of a protractor – measuring and drawing both acute and obtuse angles – use of correct scale (commonsense)

e. finding missing angles – eg in a triangle

f. logical labelling of angles, < A, < BAC or BÂC

Year 3

a. properties of corresponding, alternate, supplementary, complementary, vertically opposite angles

b. finding missing angles eg transversal of parallel lines

c. construction of angles of 60°, 90°, 45°, 135° using properties of equilateral triangles and rhombuses

Year 4

    a. directions and bearings

    b. polygons – interior and exterior angles. Construction using compass, protractor

    c. finding missing angles eg in a polygon

In about half of the schools, schemes differentiated between ability levels. Some of the schools prescribed different work for each of three broad ability levels, and in others, pupils followed the same course but at different rates. Just over a third of the schemes provided some guidance about classroom organisation and methods of teaching particular mathematical topics. The absence of such guidance sometimes led teachers to emphasise the teaching of computational skills at the expense of broader aspects of mathematics. An example of guidance is shown below :

Topic	Approach
Probability	eg using 2 dice. Children to test all the ordered pairs, and to estimate the number of times a particular total will occur in a given number of throws. Experiment and compare. Children to express probability as a fraction eg the probability of the total being seven is 1/6 ; the probability of the total being six is 5/36 etc.

Only a third of the schemes discussed presentation and marking. In most schools, schemes were given to every teacher of mathematics, but in many, these were not comprehensive enough and left too much to the discretion of the individual teacher. Very often, schemes needed extending or rewriting, if they were to be useful working documents for the large number of teachers teaching the subject.

7.42 Many of the schools relied heavily on series of mathematics text books, often supplemented by books that concentrated on the practice of mechanical arithmetic. The use of the same series of text books contributed to continuity throughout many schools, but in a third of the sample, there was a change of text book series at the end of the second year. For the most part, teachers concentrated on working through the adopted series, but in some schools, they selected topics from a variety of books or introduced material of their own. In a quarter, less able children were given different sets of text books which provided a range of mathematical activities and topics.

7.43 In half of the sample, workcards and worksheets were used frequently; in a small number of schools, they formed the main bases for the mathematics course. Over four-fifths of the schools made some use of teacher-produced materials, often of satisfactory quality, and three-fifths used commercially-produced materials. Workcards and worksheets often provided practice examples to support the work done from text books. They were used by teachers for a great variety of purposes, but particularly to cater for the range of abilities within classes, occasionally to provide opportunities for individual learning, and, in only a few cases, to encourage the application of mathematics to everyday situations. At one school, for example, worksheets were used to present a variety of applications involving such material as information leaflets distributed by estate agents.

7.44 Almost all the schools need to provide more background books to enable pupils and teachers to read more widely in the subject. Few schools had collections of books on mathematics, other than sets of text books. Only a small number of schools enabled pupils to pursue mathematical interests through the provision of books on puzzles, on geometric art and model-making, and on applications of mathematics such as computing. Where such books had been bought, insufficient use was being made of them. Very few schools provided those teaching mathematics with a range of reference books, professional journals and recent publications about the teaching of the subject.

7.45 Two-fifths of the schools used electronic calculators but mostly on a modest scale. Most often, they were used to check or to perform calculations involving awkward numbers. Only occasionally were examples seen of their being used as teaching aids : to develop the idea of place value, to help in work on number patterns, to introduce square roots and to teach simple and compound interest. In one school, activities involving calculators were important and useful components in the course provided for less able pupils. Electronic calculators were actively discouraged in a number of schools where it was feared that their use would undermine pupils' competence in basic arithmetic. In some others, decisions had been taken to leave work involving calculators to the upper school, or to postpone introducing such work until each child had a calculator. At the time of the survey, only one school had a computer, a PET ; there, pupils met in a computer club at lunchtimes and some were developing their own computer programmes.

7.46 In general, the children's response to mathematics was favourable, though not often enthusiastic. Most pupils worked steadily and responsibly. Standards of work were satisfactory in three-fifths of the schools, including ten where standards were good or very good. Not surprisingly the best work done by pupils was often associated with teaching carried out by those particularly knowledgeable in the subject but the influence of such teachers tended to be confined to their own classes. Work at an appropriate level of difficulty was provided for the large proportion of children of average ability in two-thirds of the sample, but the range of work was often narrow and, in many cases, children did not have sufficient first-hand experience of applying mathematics. More able children were given work which was generally commensurate with their abilities in about half the schools, though nowhere were the most able pupils fully challenged. Less able pupils were given work of suitable difficulty in just under half the schools, but the range of work provided was often too limited.

SCIENCE

7.47 Science was a well established part of the curriculum in the survey schools. It was taught to pupils in all year groups, except in two schools where it was not taught to all first year pupils. On average, the percentage of lesson time given to the subject increased from 6 per cent for the youngest children to 10 per cent for the oldest. Some of the schools need to consider whether more time should be given to science, if their pupils are to develop an understanding of a sufficient range of ideas and be proficient in a range of scientific processes. Science was usually timetabled as a separate subject but for the youngest pupils in about a quarter of the sample, it formed part of topic work which typically included social studies, history and geography. First year pupils were often taught science by their class teachers ; older pupils were more frequently taught by teachers who spent a substantial proportion of time teaching the subject. In just over half the schools, science was taught in mixed-ability classes in all year groups ; in the remaining schools, the youngest pupils were usually taught in mixed-ability classes and the older ones in sets or streams formed according to ability.

7.48 The type of work prescribed for pupils was predominantly related to nature and biological studies in the first two years, and moved towards a greater emphasis on topics related to the physical sciences in years three and four.

7.49 Children in years one and two studied such topics as food, the senses, the growth of seeds, trees, plant life and pond life. First year children in one school had planted seeds under controlled conditions to see if light, heat and water were necessary for germination. Elsewhere pupils in these years had studied topics such as the seashore, arthropods and birds, and had collected specimens of plants and insects. Although this pattern of biological studies was common other areas of work were sometimes introduced. For example, in one school first year pupils had built their own anemometers to record wind conditions in different parts of the school grounds. In the same school, second year pupils studying air and wind had devised ways of classifying simple and compound leaves using a variety of criteria. It was noticeable that pupils of all year groups in this school could cope well with written practical instructions. Second year pupils in another school had built their own structures from straws and as a result of testing and discussion had drawn conclusions concerning the relationship between the material, length, number of straws and strength of the construction.

7.50 Pupils in years three and four were seen working on various assignments concerned with atoms and molecules ; mechanics including friction ; light, heat, sound ; electricity and magnetism. Practical activities included experiments to find out how much air the lungs hold, and glass-blowing by which pupils were able to see a relationship between the ease of blowing and the colour of the gas flame. In one school where pupils were encouraged to devise their own experiments, those in a fourth year class were using a dynamometer to measure the force required for various purposes, for example, to open a drawer, to pull a chair and to drag another pupil along the floor. In this school, science learning was characterised by the high degree of interest and involvement shown by the children.

7.51 Pupils in all the schools did some practical work, though older pupils tended to do so more frequently than younger ones. In over four-fifths of the schools children were learning to observe scientific phenomena and in about two-fifths were responding well to the range of opportunities presented. In some schools there was shrewd questioning of children by teachers to help them sharpen their observation of their own experiments. Practical work often involved children in following step-by-step instructions rather than in finding their own ways of tackling problems posed by teachers or themselves.

In only two-fifths of the schools was there evidence that pupils occasionally devised or helped to devise experiments to test out their ideas. The limited nature of the practical work in some schools was partly the result of over-dependence on workcards or worksheets which failed to provide opportunities for more open-ended enquiries. More often, teacher-directed practical work needs to be complemented by less directed, more open-ended activities where children are helped to frame questions or state problems based on their own observations ; to select from their observations those which are relevant to the problems ; to suggest patterns in what is observed ; to offer explanations of what causes these patterns ; to test their suggested explanations ; and to record what they do in their own way.

7.52 Although in many schools, children were encouraged to discuss ideas in science with one another and their teachers, and sometimes did so very effectively, their written work was often restricted because of the set formats required for recording. In a substantial number of schools dictation of notes and copying from the blackboard were major methods for imparting information. In just under half the schools, pupils wrote more freely about science. For example in one mixed-ability class in the fourth year of one school children wrote about heating copper sulphate (a substance used in medicine and horticulture) and recorded in their own way what they had learned. In addition to helping their own understanding of what they had done their writing provided the teacher with pointers as to the extent of their understanding and ways in which the work required development. The following examples were written by two children of differing abilities :

What I remember about copper sulphate

I remember when copper sulphate is heated it turns white and loses weight. This is called anhydrous copper sulphate. Anhydrous means without water because when copper sulphate is heated the heat dries off the liquid. When you put anhydrous copper sulphate with purified water it gives off heat and returns to blue copper sulphate. We collected the liquid given off the copper sulphate and tested it. We were pretty sure it was water.

The copper sulphate experiment

When we heat copper sulphate the heat is stored in the anhydrous copper sulphate in the form of energy. When we add the water to the anhydrous copper sulphate the energy is given off as heat. When we heated copper sulphate direct, it gave off a green flame. When the copper sulphate is heated it loses mass. When we put a cool object over the copper sulphate during heating, little droplets of water condensed on the object proving the fact that vapour was coming off. We know it was water because we collected some of the liquid and tested the boiling point of the liquid. It boiled at 100° centigrade therefore it must be water.

7.53 In just over half the schools, children were sometimes encouraged to select data relevant to the problems or topics under investigation, and in a similar proportion they were given opportunities to offer speculative explanations of their own observations. In one school, for example, pupils worked enthusiastically on circuit boards, devised many different circuits and offered reasonable explanations as to the differences in brightness of bulbs in different arrangements. In general, children need more opportunities to discuss work in science so that, for example, they can put forward possible explanations of phenomena or seek evidence related to the problems or topics on which they are working.

7.54 In most schools, teachers discussed relationships or patterns in the data with pupils, and in about half the sample, pupils had some opportunities to seek such relationships or patterns for themselves. In one school a class of second year children were asked to measure their height, skin area and size of feet. They then presented this information on a range of charts and discussed the variations which these demonstrated. Relationships between measurements were discussed: for example, height and size of feet were considered to see if the tallest people had the largest feet. The children were then asked if they could think of different ways of measuring feet, and they suggested area, length, width, volume and shoe size. Asked how they would measure the volume of a foot, several children recalled previous work on volume and suggested putting one foot into a bowl of water to measure the amount of water displaced. Some second year children in another school successfully related their observation of condensation from a burning candle to earlier work on weather. However, many pupils found difficulty in relating their knowledge to different situations.

7.55 Only one-third of the schools made use of the local environment for ecological investigations and other activities. In the grounds of one school, children made extensive use of the greenhouse and paved garden and studied a variety of habitats including a pond and an area left as a 'wilderness'. About a third of the schools gave pupils experience of field work, often linked with other subjects such as geography or environmental studies. One school which provided a valuable one-week residential field-trip for all first year children included walks along nature trails and visits to industrial archaeological sites as part of its well-organised programme. A small number of the schools used materials provided by museum loan services and made visits to local zoos or museums. Overall, greater use should be made of the immediate environment and of other aids such as museum facilities in the teaching of science.

7.56 In about three-fifths of the schools, pupils were learning to handle scientific apparatus effectively and safely. In some schools, pupils developed confidence through being given an early introduction to elementary laboratory procedures and having a wide range of practical experience throughout their science course. In one school, both boys and girls in year four developed good manipulative skills linking work in science with technology: following a visit to a railway museum they were shown how to blow small spheres in order to make models of Hero's steam turbine. They made several working models of the turbine and related their observations to earlier work on thermal expansion. During the course of this work, pupils obtained their equipment in an orderly manner, paid due attention to the teacher's instructions and safety precautions, put on goggles automatically when using the bunsen burners and showed good control of practical equipment.

7.57 Links were sometimes made between science and other areas such as home studies or health education ; such links were more often made in the work done by the younger pupils in topic-based assignments. In one school, however, pairs of fourth year pupils constructed models of rooms and made various electrical circuits to light them. They successfully applied their knowledge of circuits to make single and two-way switch systems and also suggested the positioning of fuses in the circuits. In very few of the schools were mathematics and science profitably linked. An example occurred in the school where the practical work involved in making models of Hero's steam turbine had been used by the teacher to reinforce simple mathematical relationships. In most of the schools more opportunities are needed for children to apply the skills and ideas developed in science to other subjects such as craft, design and technology and to use mathematics to help them understand and express scientific ideas and relationships.

7.58 To develop children's understanding of important scientific ideas and processes, they need progressively more demanding work in the three main sciences as they move through the middle school. In general, an adequate range of topics in physics and biology was taught, but the nature and extent of the chemistry component gave cause for concern in a small number of schools. However, there was a more general need to teach scientific topics in a more effective sequence ; in many schools insufficient attention was being paid to progression through the four year course.

7.59 A large majority of schools had separate schemes of work in science except in the first year where three-fifths of schools had separate schemes and one-fifth had schemes which included science as part of larger subject combinations. Many schools used, and often modified, schemes resulting from national projects such as the Nuffield Combined Science and Schools Council Science 5 – 13 projects. Nearly all the schemes placed most emphasis upon the content to be taught, a third discussed the development of skills and a similar proportion referred to resources and teaching methods. Very few gave explicit attention to progression or to how material might be differentiated for children of different abilities. In some areas, teachers from several schools had had meetings with local advisers to produce science guidelines which gave detailed advice about content, processes, resources, teaching methods, organisation and continuity. Where these were implemented they made a valuable contribution to the quality of pupils' learning.

7.60 43 schools had science laboratories and the remainder had science areas supplied with mains services. In most schools, all third and fourth year classes used these facilities, as did all second year classes in over half the sample and all first year classes in over a quarter. Many of the youngest children were taught science in ordinary classrooms. About a third of the designated areas were small, ie less than 65 sq. m. even though some were used for the teaching of science to whole classes. Many science laboratories had poor storage facilities and few had separate preparation rooms. In about a third of the schools, services were unsatisfactory ; deficiencies included shortage of sinks, gas taps or electricity points, or sometimes all three. Whenever possible, younger children should spend some time in a properly equipped laboratory. Reasonable laboratory provision should include at least one properly equipped room of not less than 65 sq. m. Equipment should include all services, gas, water and electricity, and sufficient apparatus to carry out an appropriate range of practical work. In over four-fifths of the schools, the quality and quantity of equipment and materials were satisfactory, though in some cases inadequate supplies of electrical meters, top pan balances and microscopes limited the range of practical work that could be attempted. Where classes were taught in laboratories, many teachers and children made good use of apparatus, but much less use was made of apparatus where science was taught in ordinary classrooms. The quality and quantity of book provision were satisfactory in just under three-fifths of the sample but book resources were often under-used. Many of the schools need to improve their supply of reference books relating to physics and chemistry and to encourage children to use reference books as a normal part of their work in science.

7.61 In almost all the schools, children's attitudes to science were good and there was often lively enthusiasm in classes where learning was substantially derived from practical activities. In most schools pupils persevered with the tasks they were set but were not given many opportunities for extended work on particular topics or problems. In the few science clubs for older children enterprising and ingenious work was being attempted by some pupils. Standards of work were broadly satisfactory in almost two-thirds of the schools. The large proportion of children of average ability was given work of suitable difficulty in just over two-thirds of the sample. Much of the work given to less able pupils was appropriate in about half the schools, but abler pupils were not as well provided for ; they were given work that was judged to be commensurate with their abilities in about a third of the schools.

MODERN LANGUAGES

7.62 French was the modern language most frequently taught in the schools, though two also introduced children to a second foreign language. French was taught in all 48 schools to third and fourth year pupils. In just over half the schools, children began learning French in the first year and in all but three of the remaining schools, the language was introduced a year later. There were two streamed schools at which a substantial number of entrants were not offered French and had little chance of taking it up later. In other schools, if children did not begin to learn French, it was generally because of their need for remedial help in aspects of English. Mixed-ability classes were the normal pattern for the younger age-groups. In three-fifths of the sample, third year pupils were taught French in sets or streams according to general ability ; in the fourth year, these arrangements were employed in four-fifths of the schools. In many cases, some older, less able pupils were allowed to drop French once teachers had judged they were no longer making adequate progress. In some schools, such pupils were given extra English and in others they had background studies courses which introduced them to everyday life in France. Allowing children to drop French before the end of the course or not giving them the opportunity to learn the language leads to problems later, if pupils are required to learn French in upper schools.

7.63 In many schools, especially in the early stages of the course, listening and speaking were emphasised but in only a third of the schools did teachers develop the listening skills of their pupils by regularly using French to give instructions in the classroom. Throughout one school, however, actions such as shutting doors, opening windows, sitting and standing were all done in response to requests in French. In another school, a group of second year less able children responded well to simple instructions in a lesson during which no English was used. A small number of schools developed activities which fostered the listening comprehension of the less and the more able pupils. For example, in about a fifth of the schools bilingual communication in which the teacher used French but allowed the pupils to respond in English was regularly used to provide genuine dialogue with the less able and to develop their self confidence. Individual listening to recordings of stories to extend the listening comprehension of the more able pupils, was reported in very few classes.

7.64 A large majority of the schools introduced reading either from the beginning of the course or in its early stages, and this activity, even with the oldest pupils, consisted largely of word recognition rather than reading for understanding. To assist both their reading and their writing, pupils wrote out and learned lists of French words. Occasionally, such work involved more than just copying. For example, in one class, pupils did not copy the date from the blackboard but were required to select appropriate material from the numbers, days of the week and months of the year displayed around the room. Passages were translated either orally or as written exercises in two-thirds of the schools. Most materials, such as flash cards, displayed texts and readers, which were used to develop reading comprehension, were integral parts of published courses but in about half of the schools none was seen in use. In a similar proportion, course texts were supplemented by material of good or acceptable quality produced by teachers. Such material was generally of better quality when developed centrally by working groups of teachers who could pool their ideas.

7.65 In order to develop their ability to speak the language, pupils engaged in a variety of activities depending on their age and ability and on the teacher's approach. Repetition in French after listening to tape-recordings or to teachers was common, though such repetition sometimes resulted in inaccurate pronunciation which went unnoticed. In almost all the schools, pupils were expected to answer questions in French but in only just over a quarter were they given regular practice in asking questions in the language. In one school a class of children engaged in an exercise on tense-changing whereby, using domino-style cards, they spoke a present tense after its associated perfect. A feature of this school was children's enjoyment of French lessons and a consequence of successful teaching was that almost across the entire ability range pupils attained considerable success in comprehension and some independence in speaking and writing. In another school children spent as much time in one lesson asking questions of the teacher and of one another as they did in answering questions, but such a balance of question and response was rarely found. In only a very small number of schools were older, abler pupils required to re-tell narratives in French using their own words. Drama and role-play were sometimes used to foster competence in listening and speaking ; children were seen interviewing each other, recording dialogue on tape and acting out domestic or shopping scenes. In one class, scenes from En Avant were acted out in front of a sketch drawn on the blackboard : children brought in props, learned some of their work by heart and improvised when necessary. Activities such as singing, quizzes, guessing games and games such as 'Simon dit' were used regularly in only a minority of schools. Pronunciation and intonation were considered good in about a quarter of the schools. In over two-thirds of the schools, there was little or no progression towards independence in talking, partly because of the emphasis given to repetitive rather than creative oral exercises. In order to develop children's language, French needs to be used more regularly as the means of communication, with children encouraged to initiate conversation and to ask questions as well as to answer them.

7.66 Pupils need to be given opportunities to read not only course texts but also a range of easy readers and stories written in French, but few schools had sufficient supplementary material beyond the course text to provide appropriately for the range of reading abilities found in sets or mixed-ability groups. In one case, a teacher with special responsibility for French tackled the problem by grading his stock of French readers and designing workcards to check on children's comprehension. In another, worksheets, some containing questions in French and some questions in English, were provided to check on individual reading by pupils of different abilities. About a fifth of the schools encouraged individual reading, often for the more able once set work had been completed. It was rare to see a class reading rapidly through a chapter or a section of a class textbook before being questioned about it. In just over a third of the schools, there was evidence of progression in reading, usually as a result of children working through prescribed courses. In only a few schools, however, were pupils of all abilities given appropriate reading tasks.

7.67 There was little evidence of independent written work by children, even abler ones. Only a very limited amount of guided composition was seen. Two-thirds of the schools did not do this and only five made frequent use of the activity. In one school where abler children in the fourth year regularly wrote guided compositions, they showed they could enjoy this work and could cope well with three tenses. Occasionally, able pupils were asked to write continuous prose based on their memory of topics previously met. There were some good examples of continuous writing from older, abler children on topics such as getting up in the morning and a letter to a friend. In nearly all the schools, the children's main writing task was the completion of textbook exercises. Though in most schools success of some kind in the writing was noted, in very few cases was there adequate planned progress appropriate to various levels of ability in this difficult language skill.

7.68 There was little evidence that background studies played an important part in French teaching in the schools. Such studies could frequently have done more to increase children's motivation and to help them appreciate aspects of the French way of life. Although there were numerous examples of attractive displays of posters, newspapers, postcards and maps, these were rarely referred to in lessons seen. Just under half the schools had collections of articles from France but few made regular use of background books or French magazines. Film strips and slides were used in almost three-fifths of the schools, usually as an integral part of the course, but little use was made of radio or television programmes to introduce children to aspects of the French way of life. Some schools made good use of the knowledge gained by teachers and pupils as a result of visits to France ; fewer than one school in eight had the services of a French assistant (e).

7.69 Just over half the schools made regular arrangements for parties of pupils to visit France. The majority of such visits were for longer than a day. Another quarter had either arranged such visits in the past or had plans to do so. Such school journeys were most often for third and fourth year pupils. Correspondence with French schools, involving the exchange of tapes or letters, was noted in only four instances. Camping holidays in France appeared to provide only limited opportunities for French language development.

7.70 Within the schools, the emphasis given to the skills of listening, reading, speaking and writing depended mainly on the judgement of individual teachers rather than on policies agreed by all the staff teaching the subject. Such policies need to be drawn up as a matter of urgency and periodically reviewed to see whether appropriate emphasis is being given to each of the four language skills in the work provided for children of different abilities. Schemes of work had been drawn up in all except five schools but few were useful working documents ; about half did no more than relate the work of the various year groups to the stages of courses in use. Those that were more detailed were heavily loaded with vocabulary and grammatical content and few made reference to language skills, resources or teaching methods.

7.71 In four-fifths of the schools En Avant was the course mainly used in the early stages. A variety of secondary school courses were also used, often with older pupils but sometimes, inappropriately, with all the children learning the language. In an attempt to cater for differences in pupils' abilities, a quarter of the schools which taught French in sets switched to courses believed by the teachers to be less demanding of their older, less able pupils. Basic material for chosen courses was in reasonable supply, as were projectors and tape recorders where these were needed for the audio-visual course in use. Ten schools had more elaborate facilities for individual or group listening but in most of these, little use was made of this provision.

7.72 The general standard of work in French was fair in about half the schools though in many, there were shortcomings in the teaching of particular skills, especially writing. The work was generally suitable for the large proportion of pupils of average ability in 27 of the schools. About a third of the schools provided abler pupils with work of suitable difficulty in specific language skills but only in a few did such children achieve an appropriate level of independence in speaking and writing. Twenty schools provided satisfactorily for less able pupils, but in the remainder, reading and writing were often over-emphasised at the expense of listening and speaking.

MUSIC

7.73 Music was part of the curriculum in all the middle schools in the survey and in most of them a variety of musical activities were provided in which children could participate. Instrumental teaching, choirs, orchestras, music festivals and activities in class gave children opportunities to identify and experience the basic elements of music, to acquire the necessary skills, to participate in musical activities, and to use music as a medium for the expression of their own ideas and feelings.

7.74 About two-thirds of the schools gave adequate time overall to music, but in general less time was allocated for older children than younger ones.

Variations of time allocation usually reflected either the school's curricular priorities or particular staffing shortages in this subject. Music was usually taught to boys and girls in mixed-ability classes, but was taught to whole year groups at a time in a few schools. In addition to class work in music, teachers in three-quarters of the schools arranged extra-curricular activities such as choirs, music productions, orchestras and concert-going. Two-thirds of the sample made some special provision for musically able pupils, usually in the form of instrumental teaching, supported by extra-curricular activities. In a quarter of the schools, a few children were selected to attend local education authority centres for further instrumental tuition.

7.75 Singing was practised regularly by all pupils in over half the sample (Table 14). In almost all the schools, folk songs, sea shanties and spirituals were sung. Just under half the schools used BBC radio song material and a smaller proportion included songs from pop cantatas, musicals and other contemporary music. However, only a quarter had a repertoire of songs appropriate to pupils' age, interests or needs ; in the remainder, older children were often given a limited range of material and in some cases had few opportunities to sing. In only just over a quarter of the schools were vocal skills practised regularly and help given to children in techniques of phrasing, breathing and diction. In these schools, the quality and development of the singing were satisfactory, but this was not the case in the remainder where the acquisition of vocal skills was left to chance, the range of songs offered was often limited, and expectations were sometimes set too low. In addition to singing in class, choral activities were usually provided in schools for interested pupils ; in about three-quarters of the schools children from all year groups were members of choirs. In the most successful of these, children were singing complete choral works, often in association with dramatic productions and music festivals.

7.76 In almost four-fifths of the schools teachers made some use of instruments during music lessons, but only in 16 were they used extensively on a regular basis for group instrumental playing and as accompaniments to singing. The reading of music was regularly practised in almost two-fifths of the sample, mainly in association with recorder or other instrumental playing. The emphasis placed on this varied between year groups but in a quarter of schools no teaching of music reading was undertaken. In just under half the schools children played the recorder as a classroom activity but guitar playing and other forms of music making were less common. Instrumental playing in assembly was a regular feature in some schools and ranged from the school orchestra or band to small recorder, guitar or percussion groups. Overall, however, not enough time was given to the teaching of instrumental skills in classroom music ; positive and regular practice produced a reasonable development of such skills in only a quarter of the schools. To enable more children to participate in music-making, more attention needs to be given in class to helping pupils acquire and practise appropriate instrumental and music-reading skills. This will usually require an adjustment in the balance of the curriculum to achieve a more practical emphasis rather than any substantial increase in the time allocated to the subject.

7.77 In just over half of the schools, pupils were given some opportunities to devise their own music but in only a few was this a regular feature of the curriculum. In these, activities varied from group 'creative' music-making to arrangements of accompaniments to songs. More commonly than at present, children should be encouraged to devise their own music, whether in the form of original compositions, improvisations or arrangements of existing music.

7.78 In almost two-fifths of the schools children in all year groups were given regular opportunities to develop a critical appreciation of music ; a small number of other schools fostered this appreciation with some pupils, usually the younger ones. The successful schools encouraged children to listen critically as part of broad, well-planned programmes which involved the playing of instruments, singing, and listening to records. It was common for teachers to give introductory talks, after which recorded music was played and discussed. In one lesson, for example, the teacher introduced a record of music by Smetana by explaining its context and using the piano to isolate its melodies. While the record was being played, a film strip was shown and this was followed by discussion when the teacher again used the piano to illustrate particular points. Some schools chose a composer for the week whose work was played several times, prior to assembly and during lessons, and also discussed in class. In more schools, regular opportunities need to be provided for pupils to listen to various kinds of music and to discuss it critically.

7.79 46 schools provided instrumental teaching for small groups of children. In almost half, peripatetic teachers were responsible for all the tuition, but in the remainder school staff also participated in the teaching. In about three-fifths of the schools children were withdrawn from classes on a rota basis for tuition ; this arrangement was combined with teaching at lunch times in a further fourteen schools. Children had opportunities to learn instruments such as the violin, recorder, clarinet, trumpet, cello or guitar. Overall, about 10 per cent of second year pupils were learning instruments compared with 7 per cent of first and third year pupils and only 4 per cent of the oldest age group. Of the pupils taught by peripatetic teachers, the majority started to learn instruments in their first year at middle school, commonly in groups of between two and five pupils ; it was rare to find pupils beginning to learn instruments in the upper two years of the schools. In more than half the schools in which instruments were taught, the majority of pupils, having started instrumental lessons, continued their tuition throughout their middle school course. However, in the remaining schools, the proportion of children who ceased to have tuition, gave some cause for concern. Generally, pupils who had opportunities to use their individual musical skills in the context of ensemble, orchestral or other group work were less likely to discontinue instrumental tuition.

7.80 In many schools, groups of children who could play instruments practised regularly under the guidance of teachers. In about half the schools, second, third and fourth year pupils played in school orchestras ; the proportion of schools involving first year children was slightly lower. First year children were members of recorder groups in over three-quarters of the schools but recorders were played by older children in a somewhat smaller proportion of the sample. Pupils who had the opportunity to progress to tenor and base recorders and to experience a wide range of the recorder repertoire found the work rewarding and sometimes achieved commendable standards.

7.81 To support the work in music, all but three schools had schemes of work. Content, skills and resources were given detailed attention in two-fifths of the schemes and limited attention in over one-fifth. Less consideration was given to teaching methods and organisation and only one in three of the schemes drew attention to progression. Schemes were followed fairly closely in two-thirds of the sample.

7.82 Almost every school had a designated teaching area where most of the music teaching took place. In a quarter of schools this was either a purpose-built specialist music room or a specialist room formed by adaptations to existing buildings. The accommodation provided for class music teaching was considered suitable for the work undertaken in over half the schools and included purpose-built, modified and ordinary classrooms. In over half of the schools there was no separate storage space for instruments or other musical equipment. In the remainder the provision ranged from good walk-in storerooms to satisfactory storage arrangements. Accommodation for instrumental teaching was poor : less than a third of the schools had satisfactory rooms and over half had no practice rooms available for individual teaching.

Table 14 *The balance of the music curriculum*

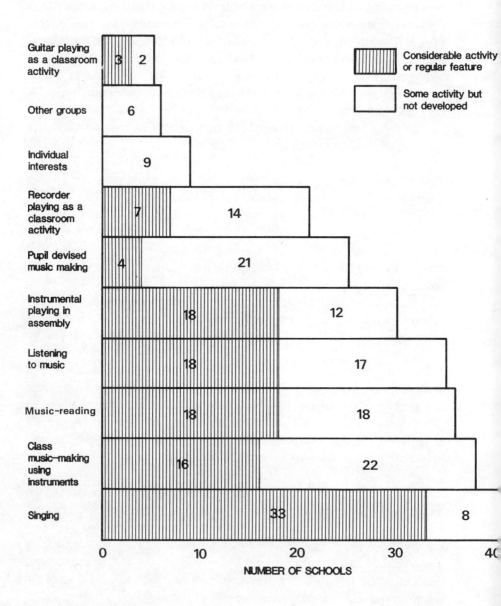

7.83 Resources for music teaching varied widely, from schools with a few resources, to those which had many classroom instruments, orchestral and band instruments, a varied supply of audio-visual equipment, and plentiful textbooks, song books and worksheets. Overall, about three-fifths of the sample had equipment and materials which were satisfactory in both quantity and quality.

7.84 The standards of work in just over half the schools were broadly satisfactory, though they varied from one aspect of the music curriculum to another. The large proportion of children of average ability was given suitable work in about half of the schools. Just under half provided appropriately for less able children, but more able pupils were not as well provided for : their needs were satisfactorily met in about a third of the sample. In general, younger children tended to be given more suitable work than older ones. There were indications that boys were less involved in the work than girls. None of the schools were able, during school time, to make entirely satisfactory provision for exceptionally talented children, but extra tuition was sometimes provided in out-of-school hours.

ARTS AND CRAFTS

Timetable arrangements

7.85 All the schools provided opportunities for children to acquire knowledge of materials and to develop a variety of skills in their use. In many of the schools, art was timetabled separately from craft activities but in a substantial minority of schools, both areas of work were incorporated into large subject combinations which appeared on the timetables under various headings such as design, practical subjects or craft. Aspects of the work related to art and design, to needlecrafts, to home studies, and to craft, design and technology, were inspected as separate components whatever the timetable arrangements employed.

7.86 Art was part of the curriculum in all 48 schools, and aspects of craft, design and technology were taught in 39. Rather more schools timetabled both these areas of work as separate subjects than as part of subject combinations. In about two-thirds of the schools, they were taught as part of rotational patterns of activities. In most cases, such patterns involved home studies and needlecrafts as well as art, and craft, design and technology. Needlecrafts were taught in almost every school but in some, the subject was not timetabled for some year groups.

Art and design

7.87 Art was taught to all children, usually in mixed-ability classes. In a few schools boys and girls were taught separately for part of the work. Drawing and painting were common activities. Pencil, crayon, charcoal, powder colour and poster colour were widely used, but less use was made of media such as water colour or oil paint. In many schools, pottery and clay modelling were important aspects of art but only in a few cases was work fired or glazed. Block printing and, to a lesser extent, screen and fabric printing were also taught. Fabric work such as tie dye, collage, batik, weaving and embroidery was provided in a smaller number of schools. Few schools included carving or used paper and card for three-dimensional constructions.

7.88 Children were frequently asked to look at natural and man-made objects but were not always taught to observe them carefully and thoroughly as part of the process of recording them in a variety of media. Good observation was encouraged in one school where pupils in the first year were introduced to drawing leaves, twigs and bark ; this observational work extended in the second year to include a range of man-made objects. In the remaining two years, children used charcoal, paint, and pen and ink to record their observations of landscapes and of objects such as bones and skulls. Elsewhere teachers had used museum loan services to provide objects for study and drawing, for example a fox, duck, snake, lizard and butterflies. One art teacher had brought her own live pet pheasant in a cage for pupils to draw. In another school, where children were drawing a spider plant, the teacher fostered observation by encouraging pupils to pay attention to points such as the proportion of the plant-holder to the plant, the structure of the plant's roots and the shape and fall of the leaves. In the third and fourth years of one school children looked closely at sections of vegetables and fruit such as cucumbers and oranges and subsequently used the patterns observed to form the basis of lino prints and screen printing. However, there is a need, in many of the schools, for children to be taught to observe more carefully, to select with discrimination and to record their observations accurately and sensitively.

7.89 In many cases greater and more effective use might be made of the immediate environment as a source of first-hand experience and a stimulus for work in art. Only a third of the schools were using the environment in this way. Effective use of the environment and its resources was illustrated in one school where visits were made to local museums, drawings of buildings were based on first-hand experience, and an art week involving local artists was arranged. An art teacher in the same school displayed his personal prints which were used to stimulate art work and illustrate different styles used by artists. One consequence of this provision was that pupils were able to talk with knowledge about a range of artistic experience.

7.90 Almost all schools gave some attention to display. Over a third of the schools had displays of a quality which helped pupils' appreciation of art and enhanced the environment.

7.91 In many of the schools, pupils were developing an awareness of colour, shape, form, pattern and movement. This awareness was more frequently apparent in relation to colour, tone, shape and composition, and less so in relation to pattern and texture. In more of the schools, children need to be encouraged to develop this awareness and more analysis of objects or first-hand experiences would assist it. In this way they would be helped to understand the language necessary to describe, analyse and discuss art, whether produced by themselves or by practising artists.

7.92 Through the handling of tools and equipment in printing, painting, clay work and other activities, pupils were using a variety of manipulative skills. In one school where pupils were systematically taught the care and handling of tools and equipment, these skills were gradually consolidated and children became quite expert in selecting appropriate instruments, particularly in painting. However, in many schools the extension of such skills was not often evident, as few children were given enough time or help in handling tools, to work with different media or to produce different effects with the same medium. During the four year course children need to be given opportunities to acquire a degree of mastery of essential skills and techniques used in a range of two- and three-dimensional work.

7.93 In ten schools, pupils were given opportunities to make judgements within the constraints of design problems. In one example of such work children drew a display of objects which reflected light, and were then set the problem of designing the support of a source of light and incorporating some form of reflector in their design. Most children used wood, metal and ceramics to make candle-holders with inset or separate reflectors. Generally, more work calling for solutions to simple design problems could be attempted.

7.94 Teaching which encouraged children to discriminate, make judgements and express opinions about their own work and that of others was observed in only a small number of schools. In many classes, general discussion of the work was not encouraged and children often lacked an appropriate vocabulary with which to discuss art. A small number of schools were achieving a measure of success in developing pupils' judgement. In one, pupils were articulate about their experiences and able to give constructive comments on modifications made to the tasks in hand. In another, at the end of a lesson when three-dimensional designs had been completed, children were invited to comment on the work produced, in terms of the choice and use of paper and card, the colours used, the effectiveness of shapes and the balance achieved. The discussion contributed to the development of discrimination and judgement which were marked features of the work in the upper part of this school. In many schools, children's critical awareness of their own work and that of established artists and designers could be stimulated by the use of suitable reference books and by more opportunities for extended discussion.

7.95 In many schools, pupils worked carefully within closely prescribed limits. In half the sample, they were given adequate opportunities to produce work showing personal interpretation but in only a small number of schools was such work strongly encouraged and developed. In one case, personal interpretation was fostered throughout the school, especially in the third and fourth years. Expressive activities included drawing buildings in the locality, painting aspects of the local environment on paper and on rough canvas, work with clay, collage, and craft work involving moving cog wheels. In some schools, however, children were not given sufficient opportunities for close observation, for selection of materials, and for the exercise of inventiveness and personal interpretation. Such opportunities could be offered more widely in relation to work in three dimensions as well as in two.

7.96 To support the work in art, almost all the schools had schemes of work or guidelines but in only a quarter of the schools was there evidence of their being used. Two-thirds of the schemes were concerned with art as a separate subject rather than as part of a larger subject combination such as design. Schemes emphasised the development of skills, but few made reference to teaching methods or the development of ideas. Available resources were frequently listed but there were few references to safety factors.

7.97 All but three schools had designated teaching areas where most of the teaching of art took place. The youngest pupils were more likely than others to be taught art in their own classrooms although all first year classes in two-fifths of the schools had the use of designated areas. Older age groups had progressively greater access to specialised facilities and in over two-thirds of schools, all fourth year classes used designated areas. Frequently, such areas were used for wood and metal crafts as well as for art, pottery and fabric work. In half the schools, the accommodation was satisfactory, that is, having adequate space, with good lighting and appropriate ventilation and storage facilities, but in the remainder, there were unsatisfactory features such as poor lighting, inadequate storage facilities, inappropriate furnishings, or multiple use which, to some extent, impeded aspects of the work.

7.98 In just over two-thirds of the schools, equipment and consumable materials used for art were satisfactory both in quantity and quality. Generally, however, book provision was less adequate. Wall charts and photographs were used in rather more than a fifth of the schools and about a third of the schools made some use of film strips or slides. In almost a third of the schools, teachers' own collections of reference material were referred to, but only in a few instances was use made of pupils' own collections.

7.99 In almost half the schools, standards of work were generally satisfactory, though they were good throughout all four year groups in only a few cases. Overall, work at an appropriate level of difficulty was given to the substantial number of children of average ability in about two-fifths of the schools and to less able children in a slightly smaller proportion. In only about one-quarter of the schools were children of above average ability given suitably challenging tasks.

Craft, design and technology

7.100 In craft, design and technology (CDT) children learn about the physical and aesthetic qualities of materials, acquire the skills to shape them, and, in some cases, learn how to plan and execute work of their own design. Elements of CDT were taught in all but nine schools and almost always to both boys and girls.

7.101 In about half of the schools in the survey the work was of a satisfactory standard, though in some cases, opportunities were restricted somewhat by the limited range of materials used and the tasks set. In a small number of schools, pupils achieved high standards of craftsmanship and were able to make sound judgements when tackling practical problems. Older pupils were more likely to have opportunities to do work related to craft, design and technology, though in half the schools the younger children did some such work.

7.102 In general, children worked enthusiastically and industriously at their tasks. The large number of pupils of average ability were given suitable work in about half the schools teaching the subject, but in the remainder, their ideas and skills were not being extended sufficiently. Tasks and approaches were modified, not always successfully, for less able children in just under half the schools teaching the subject and for abler pupils in about a quarter.

7.103 In two-thirds of the schools, the work was characterised by an emphasis on the acquisition and practice of basic manipulative skills. In most of these schools, work was done mainly in response to step-by-step instructions but in some, children made some decisions about the nature of their work, particularly about the techniques and materials to be employed. In almost a third of the schools, children were taught manipulative skills but were also expected to make decisions as to the organisation of their work, the selection of appropriate tools and the interpretation of the task in hand. Pupils were encouraged, in some schools, to discuss the development of their work with one another and the teacher, but in very few was adequate attention given to discussion and judgements about products, or an exploration of the design problems encountered. In most schools, safe habits of working were fostered through satisfactory organisation, supervision and demonstration.

7.104 Wood was the most common resistant material used in the schools. Most schools made use of soft wood, hard wood and wood products and many used scrap wood which sometimes restricted the kind of work that could be attempted. Children learned the basic techniques of marking out, cutting, glueing and nailing. Drilling machines were used by pupils in 12 schools, and disc-sanders and wood-turning lathes were each used in 6. In a quarter of the schools, metal was used, mainly in the form of thin sheet copper, tin-plate and brass. Techniques taught included marking out, hollowing, soldering and cutting. In a few cases, the work extended to the enamelling of copper shapes and the use of a metal-turning lathe. Pupils designed copper and aluminium bowls and pieces of jewellery ; in one school, the work included enamelling, engraving patterns of letters and making pendants from copper. In two schools, plastic in the form of thin acrylic sheet was also being used. The introduction of work involving metal or plastic might be considered in a greater number of the schools.

7.105 Craft, design and technology should give children opportunities to work on design tasks through the analysis of problems, the devising and sketching of alternative solutions, the selection of materials and processes, and the production of completed items. Sketching as an integral part of the design process was taught in only 7 schools, though in a similar number, formal technical drawing was taught, usually in the final year. In many schools, no purposeful drawing of sketch diagrams or illustrations was seen. Except in a small number of schools, there was little evidence of pupils being given tasks which required them to analyse problems and make forms or structures which made use of these analyses. In one school activity in craft led on to work in science. Some third year pupils were asked to design and construct a helter-skelter marble run out of card. When they had made it, they went on to experiment with varying the angle of the run to increase the speed of the marbles. They designed various chutes in an attempt to ensure that the marbles followed the curves, rather than fell off, and they designed a variety of fielding devices at the foot of the helter-skelter. In addition to directed work aimed at the development of skills, children need more opportunities to reach their own decisions about the design of articles they are going to make and about the materials, tools and techniques needed to produce them. In particular, work of a technological kind involving the design and making of things that work needs to be introduced.

7.106 More often, skills and ideas learned in craft, design and technology could be applied in other areas of the curriculum. In only a small number of the schools were elements of craft and design incorporated in topic work or related strongly to work in art.

7.107 The majority of schools had schemes of work or guidelines, though some of these did not refer to work for the youngest pupils. Content in the schemes was generally limited to a description of manipulative skills or basic techniques for handling materials and to lists of items to be made using these techniques. Skills involved in design featured in only a minority of schemes, as did references to pupils making decisions and trying out their own ideas.

7.108 Almost all the schools in the sample had areas designated for work in craft, design and technology. These areas were supplied with electricity and water, and most were adequately provided with working surfaces. In most, some form of machinery was included either for pupil or teacher use but in some cases, machinery needed to be better maintained. A wide range of hand-tools was available in about half the schools. Many schools did not have adequate storage facilities for materials and for work in hand and many lacked space for the display of three-dimensional work. About two thirds of the sample had equipment suitable in quantity and quality, but in some cases this was unused because there was no teacher with the appropriate technical expertise. In about two-thirds of the schools, the quality and quantity of materials were satisfactory. In the majority of schools, there was a lack of books to support the work, but where books were available, they were rarely used. Greater use could have been made of out-of-school resources. In particular, more needed to be done to increase children's awareness of the role of design and technology in a modern society by making contacts with local industries and crafts.

7.109 Compared with woodwork or metal work, craft, design and technology is a recent development. Many schools need to reconsider their programmes of work to see if boys and girls in all year groups could be given opportunities to work with materials such as wood, metal or plastic. In many of the schools, clearer expectations are needed concerning the abilities to be developed by craft, design and technology, the range of activities to be included and the material provision required to sustain such work. These expectations need to be incorporated into guidelines drawn up in consultation with advisers and with all the staff involved in teaching this area of the middle school curriculum.

Needlecrafts

7.110 Needlecrafts were taught in almost every school but in some were not provided for the younger pupils. Most often, needlecrafts appeared separately on the timetable or as part of home studies, but were sometimes incorporated into wider curricular areas such as design or arts and crafts. In most of the schools, needlecrafts were taught to boys and girls in their normal mixed-ability classes, though in six schools the subject was taught to girls but not boys in the fourth year. In these schools, boys and girls need to have a similar range of opportunities to work in needlecrafts.

7.111 In many schools, much of the work was closely directed by teachers and gave children few opportunities to take decisions, or solve problems.

Because of the high cost of fabric, teachers often cut out material for their pupils instead of allowing them to do it for themselves. More opportunities are needed for children to solve design problems through discussion and trying things out for themselves using less expensive materials.

7.112 In some of the schools, where there was a high level of expectation on the part of the teachers, the work in fabric and thread was of high quality and showed that children were developing an awareness of colour, texture and design. Some schools had taken children's personal interests into account, and in consequence they often worked with great enthusiasm. In one class, for example, a group of boys were making bags for fishing rods and the girls were making their own skirts. In another class, a group of boys were making and tie-dyeing tee-shirts and were engrossed in their work. Some work was done incidentally in needlecrafts to encourage children to care for their clothes and personal possessions, but generally in the schools more emphasis could be given to consideration of the cost of clothes, textiles and sewing equipment.

7.113 Children were usually taught to handle tools and equipment safely. They usually cooperated readily in the sharing of materials and equipment but were not given many opportunities for cooperative work in small groups. In one class, a small number of pupils were encouraged to plan and put up a display of finished articles on the theme 'Wheels within wheels' ; this showed a good understanding of contrast related to colour, shape and texture. In another class, second year pupils were using sewing machines to prepare small 'self-portraits' which were appliqued on to hessian squares to make a group collage.

7.114 In just under half the schools, links were fostered between work in needlecrafts and work in other subjects. In many schools, lessons on fabric printing and tie-dyeing were followed up in needlecrafts where the printed material was made into toys and other articles. Links with science were less frequent, though in one school pupils had investigated the properties of different textiles. Visits to museums were sometimes used to stimulate interest in such activities as weaving and fabric printing. In one first year class, work in humanities involved the study of suitable clothing for winter and summer and the properties of different fabrics were discussed as well as the replacement of natural fibres by man-made fibres in recent years. In another school, a visit to the seashore led to work in English, environmental studies, art and needlecrafts. As part of the work, a group of twelve-year-old girls examined a starfish, discussed its shape and texture and tried to create the same effect with fabrics and threads of different colours and textures.

7.115 To support the work, most of the schools had schemes, more often for needlecrafts as a separate subject than as part of a larger subject combination. The majority of these schemes emphasised the acquisition of skills, including those needed to operate sewing machines. Many of them included details of the articles to be made and the stitches to be included. Topics frequently mentioned were creative embroidery, toy-making, picture-making, choice of fabrics and dressmaking processes. Resources, teaching methods and organisation were referred to in a small number of schemes. Little explicit consideration was given to progression, although, in practice, a progression of activities, in terms of difficulty, was usually provided.

7.116 Almost four-fifths of the schools had designated teaching areas where most of the teaching of needlecrafts took place. Areas which provided good lighting, ventilation, hot and cold water, and conveniently placed storage facilities and which would accommodate the required number of pupils and allow for appropriate supervision were considered the most satisfactory. In most schools, the areas were also used for the teaching of home studies and, in a few cases, art and craft. In the majority of areas, work surfaces were clean and in good condition, though there were problems with dust in some open-plan accommodation. In such settings work in needlecrafts needed to be sited away from activities where children were working with wood or metal. Some designated areas contained good displays of plants, commercial posters and examples of pupils' work such as glove puppets, toys, collage and patchwork. Where ordinary classrooms were used for teaching needlecrafts, storage facilities for machines and materials were sometimes unsatisfactory. In all, approximately a third of the rooms, sometimes with minor reservations, were considered to be appropriate for the teaching of this subject.

7.117 Just over half the sample had equipment which was satisfactory in quality and quantity for the work being undertaken. In general, the maintenance of tools and machinery was satisfactory. Half the schools had adequate supplies of materials for the work planned. Normally children were required to purchase large pieces of fabric but were not charged for smaller fabric pieces used in patchwork, collage or similar activities. Stocks of background books in many schools required improvement, especially those suitable for less able and younger children ; only about a quarter of the schools had enough good quality reference books to support the work being undertaken. Few books were seen to be used in connection with needlecraft studies in any of the schools visited. A small number of schools had made visits in connection with work in needlecrafts ; these included visits to a tweed mill, a local weaver and a fashion show at a local polytechnic.

7.118 Standards of work in needlecrafts were satisfactory or better in about two-fifths of the schools. Less able children were given suitable work in two-fifths of the sample. Although in half the schools, children of above average ability were sometimes given appropriate work, it was unusual for abler pupils to have work which regularly challenged and extended their skills and understanding.

HOME STUDIES

7.119 Home studies is a subject intended to help children acquire knowledge, skills and attitudes which will enable them to make a more thoughtful and effective contribution to home and family life. In some studies children learn about the significance of food in family life ; learn how to prepare various kinds of food, and learn about the simple rules of nutrition and the link between food and health. In some of the survey schools home studies also included needlecrafts. Although elements of home studies are taught in primary schools, the subject is more firmly established in middle schools where it is usually provided for both boys and girls, often as part of a rotational pattern of activities. In almost every school in the survey, home studies was timetabled for third and fourth year pupils. In over two-thirds of these schools it was taught to second year children, and in half, to first year pupils. In most schools, the older pupils were taught by teachers who spent much of their time teaching the subject. In some cases, the younger children were taught by such teachers and in others, by their class teachers or by other members of staff who took a small number of classes for the subject. In about three-quarters of the schools, boys and girls were usually taught together in mixed-ability classes. In the remainder of the schools, all the boys and girls were timetabled separately for the subject, and in some cases, girls were given more time for these studies than were boys. In these schools, boys and girls need to be given similar opportunities in home studies and to be taught together whenever possible.

7.120 Demonstration by the teacher followed by practical work was a common feature of the work in home studies. It was unusual to find variation in the type of activities which allowed for the range of abilities within a class.

Much of the work was closely teacher-directed and the children were given only limited opportunities to make decisions. Though the cost of materials constrain the work undertaken, pupils need to acquire more than simple cooking skills and to be given opportunities to experiment with, and to investigate the properties of, materials and to try out things for themselves.

7.121 In the majority of the schools, pupils were taught to use materials economically. Teachers emphasised the cost and encouraged children to be aware of fluctuating prices of food and to compare costs in local shops and markets. In one school first year pupils visited the school canteen, talked to the cook about that day's lunch and the quantities of food needed to make the required number of meals. Often however, children missed the opportunity to cost the ingredients they were using because these had been brought ready weighed from home. In one useful lesson, children compared cakes made by traditional methods with cakes made from commercial package mixes and cakes purchased from a shop ; they discussed the flavour, texture, time expended and value for money. In another example, where pupils made a pizza, its value as a balanced meal was discussed together with its costs and ingredients from which it was made. Emphasis was given to the use of herbs and flavourings and to the most suitable tools and equipment to use for various processes.

7.122 In almost all the schools, children learned how to handle kitchen tools and domestic equipment confidently and safely. Only seven examples were noted of insufficient care being taken in the use of cutting tools. In almost all schools the importance of hygiene was stressed : in handling food, in laundering linen and in keeping work surfaces and equipment clean. Pupils usually wore appropriate protective clothing for practical work. In half the schools, children were taught how to care for their clothes and personal possessions.

7.123 In a number of schools teachers prepared worksheets which encouraged and assisted children to extract information from leaflets and reference books. In one school, some children continued their topic work on health during the holiday and on their own initiative visited a local clinic, interviewed an environmental health officer and later wrote up their findings in a question and answer style.

7.124 In many of the schools children learned to work quickly, effectively and to time. In some lessons, before they began preparing meals, children made simple plans to encourage the wise use of time. Some fourth year pupils were given opportunities to organise their own practical work and to use automatic timers on cookers. In general, children worked conscientiously, tidied up appropriately and cooperated in the sharing of equipment, materials and space.

7.125 In a number of schools common topics such as the digestive system, food tests and plant and animal reproduction were discussed separately in science and in home studies. In one school the teachers concerned with home studies and science were timetabled together for the whole of the year group and this resulted in cooperative planning, teaching and record keeping. In another school, pupils examined yeast and then experimented with it to discover the effects of temperature change. They discussed the content and suitability of different varieties of flour and then applied this knowledge by making various kinds of bread. In some schools where there was an agreed policy for health education, there was close collaboration between the teacher with special responsibility for home studies and other staff involved, such as teachers of physical education. Hygiene and nutrition were sometimes dealt with in both areas of the curriculum but in a complementary, not repetitive, way. Simple nutrition was introduced to second year pupils in one school and pupils discussed the presence of vitamin C in some fruit and vegetables. Another school had built on children's interest by discussing foods and menus for a forthcoming camping holiday.

7.126 In a few schools, opportunities were taken to link work in home studies with some of the work in humanities. In one case, a topic on India involved some fourth year children in using reference books and others in making a variety of curries. The curries were displayed on an attractively laid table together with dishes of the appropriate accompaniments supplied by the teacher. When all the food had been cooked, the pupils gathered together to discuss the work. The discussion ranged over flavour, garnish, colour, reasons for eating curries in hot countries and the place of curries in the diet of people living in India and in Britain. In another example, the topic 'Food in Victorian times' included written work in the classroom and practical activity in the home studies area. Pupils made gruel and soda bread, which they ate and compared with present day foods. In many schools there were no specifically planned links, and although much of the work in humanities was concerned with aspects of home studies such as clothes, food or family life, opportunities to reinforce learning through practical activities were not sufficiently recognised.

7.127 Home studies contributed to the development of children's mathematical understanding mainly by providing opportunities for pupils to estimate and to weigh materials and to measure liquids. In one school, as part of their work in mathematics children made a survey of the local shops, found out the shopping habits of different age groups and recorded their findings in graphical form. In most schools there was insufficient recognition by teachers of the value of extended discussion. Pupils learned to read and interpret written and oral instructions, but the writing was generally limited to copied notes or recipes. In many of the schools, work in home studies needed to be planned to allow time for activities to be discussed thoroughly and for children to write more freely about their practical work.

7.128 All schools but two had schemes of work for home studies, usually as a separate subject rather than as part of a larger subject combination. Most schemes detailed the content to be covered emphasising the cooking of isolated dishes but also considering nutrition, hygiene, safety in the home and food sources. The majority also laid emphasis on practical activities in food preparation and on manipulative skills needed to handle equipment safely. Reference to teaching methods was a common feature, but resources and general ideas which pupils might acquire were mentioned infrequently. In the schemes little explicit attention was given to progression, but in practice a progression of activities was usually provided. About half the schools followed their schemes closely ; a high proportion of these with good results.

7.129 With the exception of one all-boys' school, every school in the sample had accommodation for home studies. In about two-thirds of the schools, the room or area was also used for the teaching of needlecrafts. In most cases, the accommodation was satisfactory, though only a minority of schools had good storage provision or dining or laundry facilities. In some open-plan settings, the accommodation was poorly sited and there were problems of noise and dust from craft areas. To prevent the contamination of food, the siting and possible screening off of activities involving food preparation needs to be considered. In some of the schools, the areas used for home studies contained good displays of plants, fresh and dried flowers, carefully selected commercially published material and examples of pupils' work. A few had interesting displays on particular aspects of the work such as one on Victorian household equipment. Some schools had facilities for cooking in class bases, usually in addition to provision in designated areas. In the large majority of schools, all classes who were taught home studies had access to the designated teaching areas.

7.130 In most schools, there was sufficient equipment for home studies, although in about one-fifth lack of provision restricted the range of practical work which could be undertaken. The quality of equipment was satisfactory in two-thirds of the schools. In general, the siting and maintenance of equipment of all kinds were satisfactory. In most schools, children brought their own ingredients for cooking sessions ; arrangements were usually made for those children who were unable to provide such materials. Book provision was less satisfactory than the provision of equipment or consumable materials ; many schools needed to improve their stock of books, especially for less able and for younger pupils. In some schools, teachers made extensive use of duplicated recipe sheets. In a small number of schools teachers had prepared their own work cards, many of which were well-presented and adapted to suit different levels of ability within their classes. Little use was made of television programmes or film strips. A small number of schools had taken groups of children to museums or other local places of interest specifically in connection with work in home studies. Eight schools, for example, had visited gas or electricity board showrooms for demonstrations of equipment.

7.131 Standards of work in home studies were judged to be satisfactory in two-thirds of the schools. In a small number of these, standards were good throughout and in the others varied with different age groups or ability levels. Generally, however, the range of work was narrowly conceived and concentrated on cooking skills. Work of appropriate difficulty was provided for the large number of children of average ability in half of the schools. Less able pupils were given suitable work in two-fifths of the sample. In only a quarter of the schools were children of above average ability given suitably challenging work ; there was little differentiation between the content of the work, teaching approaches and pace for able pupils and those for pupils of average or below average ability. However, in a small number of schools, activities were planned and organised so that abler pupils extended their work individually and made many of their own decisions ; for example in selecting a recipe, deciding on the correct consistency of a mixture, or judging when food was cooked.

PHYSICAL EDUCATION

7.132 Physical education was taught in all the schools in the survey. It was seen by them as an important part of the middle school curriculum and it provided children with opportunities to participate in a variety of activities including games, gymnastics, athletics, swimming and outdoor pursuits. Not all aspects of the subject were given equal emphasis with each year group or in each school. The programme of work included games and gymnastics at all stages but the time given to the teaching of gymnastics sometimes declined in the fourth year usually because there was a greater emphasis on games. Swimming featured in the programme of about three-fifths of the schools, mainly for the first and second year pupils, whereas dance was taught in less than half the schools. Athletics and outdoor pursuits, such as camping and hostelling, were undertaken in many schools, mostly in the summer term. Voluntary activities outside the school timetable were a prominent feature of most schools and made a major contribution to the work in physical education.

7.133 In all the schools, physical education was timetabled as a separate subject. In four-fifths, the teaching was shared between specialists and non-specialists, the latter tending to take responsibility for the indoor work of the younger classes or to share in the teaching of games. Pupils were taught in mixed-ability classes except sometimes for swimming and, sometimes, for games where groups were formed on the basis of pupils' skills. Just over half the schools did not separate the sexes for indoor work in physical education ; the remainder had single-sex classes in one or more age groups, most commonly with older pupils. For games, three-fifths of the schools separated boys and girls in all year groups ; only eight schools retained mixed classes throughout. Swimming was usually taught to mixed classes of boys and girls.

7.134 Games were taught regularly throughout the year, sometimes with an increasing emphasis as pupils grew older. The programme for all abilities and age groups centred around traditional team games such as soccer, rugby, hockey, netball, cricket and rounders. All schools except four had playing fields on site and all but one had hard playing surfaces. About half the schools had facilities for playing tennis. Maintenance of fields was generally satisfactory but the quality of pitches often hindered the playing of cricket. Many schools attempted to simplify the work for younger children by teaching introductory skills and by organising practices and games involving small groups of children. In these circumstances, there were seen to be advantages in retaining mixed classes for games so that boys and girls became versatile in a range of games skills. Out of school hours there was often a range of activities provided in addition to the traditional team games : badminton, volley-ball, basket-ball, squash and other games were reported. In the main, pupils of all abilities were hardworking, keen and appropriately dressed for games. The competitive nature of team games tended to be enjoyed by the older and more able games players. Some of the heavier, rapidly maturing girls tended to lose enthusiasm for team games as they grew older, while the boys often showed an increase in vigour, agility and capacity for exercise as they matured. Many of the schools need, in the light of pupils' physical development, to consider the balance of the programme for boys and girls towards the end of the middle years. Overall, about a third of the schools achieved work of good quality in games through carefully planned courses characterised by progression, variety of experience, opportunity for individual practice and work in small groups. In other schools, there was a need for teaching to be more systematic and for pupils to be given better opportunities to develop skills. Some indoor games sessions, for example, tended to be regarded as providing only recreation and the chance to 'let off steam'. Where there was a greater sense of purpose, however, and no undue reliance on competition to motivate pupils, both boys and girls responded with keenness and obvious enjoyment.

7.135 All schools had an indoor space for the teaching of gymnastics and in two-thirds this served as both gymnasium and assembly hall. Over three-quarters of the schools were adequately or well equipped for gymnastics teaching, though five schools were without fixed apparatus and rather more had traditional secondary apparatus which the younger children found difficult to handle. The educational benefit of training pupils to move and assemble apparatus was under-valued in about one-third of the schools. Although it was rare for approaches to be consistent across a year group or from year to year, three main approaches to the teaching of gymnastics were used. Some of the work helped children become more aware of the way they moved, through exploring themes such as modes of travel, balancing, twisting and symmetry. Other activities were linked to particular skills and included specific agilities and vaults and exercises to improve strength and stamina. Some classes engaged in miscellaneous activities, deriving from a variety of sources, which provided exercise but little development of skills or improvement in the range of movement experience. Sometimes, lessons were not arranged to allow sufficient time for apparatus to be used fully and effectively and for previous work to be applied to new situations ; this was particularly the case where lessons were limited to thirty minutes. Although the overall response of pupils in all year groups was enthusiastic and vigorous, comparatively few pupils were able to build on their early gymnastic experiences to achieve good quality movement. Often, there was an unspecific requirement to achieve variety in terms of movement without the necessary challenge to achieve progression, control and gymnastic style. Confidence in movement was being developed in three-quarters of the schools through gymnastics or games but only rarely was it accompanied by attention to sensitivity in movement. To a limited extent, this development occurred in some of the school gymnastic clubs. Good standards of work in gymnastics were associated with appropriately graded tasks, clear and systematic teaching, opportunity for the children to observe good performances, an appropriate pace, and adequate revision and practice.

7.136 Except for cross-country running in winter in a few schools, athletics was confined to the summer term when both track and field events were practised. Most pupils handled equipment for athletics safely and sensibly, but they often lacked the strength and coordination to develop competence in specialised techniques in the short time available. Insufficient allowance was made for the range of ability and the age of pupils who all tended to be given similar experiences, irrespective of their physical type and stage of development. Approaches which emphasised the encouragement of individual skills and interest in running, throwing and jumping activities seemed more appropriate than those stressing the practice of highly specialised techniques.

7.137 Though very few schools had their own swimming pool, all but ten provided swimming for at least some pupils. Tuition of first and second year children tended to be the priority, with other year groups swimming if opportunity allowed. Usually, children were grouped according to their attainment, and tuition was shared by swimming instructors and teachers. The range of work included activities to develop confidence in water, the teaching of strokes, instruction in survival methods and diving practice. By the end of the second year the majority of children could swim competently. As proficiency developed, they were often encouraged to swim increasing distances and to work for local authority and other awards, sometimes as part of club activities. In almost all the schools where swimming was seen, the children were achieving good standards.

7.138 Compared with games, gymnastics and swimming, expressive movement and dance were less frequently taught and then largely to first and second year pupils. The younger pupils were more successful than the older ones ; compared with girls, boys were frequently more ill-at-ease and lacking in confidence, but when committed to the task, were lively and imaginative. In general, the work did not develop beyond an elementary stage and there was too little teacher demonstration and intervention. Much of the work in dance was centred around a movement idea or was based on poetry, taped music or percussion. A small number of examples of good practice were seen. In one class of first and second year pupils, the lesson was based on a poem about witches. The sequence of activities was well worked out and new material was added, including experimental work on the use of percussion.

The effective use of space was emphasised and the work was developed by the teacher's sensitive use of language. A few schools included country-dancing in their programmes of work. In general, more opportunities need to be given for children to develop skill in dance and to acquire an understanding of the way movement can be used to communicate feelings and ideas.

7.139 Schools varied in the extent to which they provided opportunities for children to participate in outdoor pursuits. Opportunities ranged from an annual day trip to a programme for all age groups including walks, camps, weekend visits, longer stays at field-study centres and trips abroad, some of which stimulated later work in the classroom. In one school, fourth year pupils helped to make canoes and before using them on an expedition, practised elementary canoeing skills at the local baths. In other schools, preparatory work for expeditions, such as courses in camping techniques, took place as extra-curricular activities.

7.140 Although in many schools opportunities were not taken to relate physical education to other areas of the curriculum, some links were noted : pupils observed the effects of exercise on pulse, circulation and breathing, drew and modelled human figures, studied physical training in Victorian education, discussed the relationship between exercise and good health, and used poetry and literature as stimuli for work in dance.

7.141 With very few exceptions, pupils responded keenly and vigorously to physical education and behaved responsibly and thoughtfully. Cooperation based on friendliness and respect was expected and achieved by teachers. Children readily cooperated with one another, especially older girls who enjoyed working together in less closely supervised groups. While schools regarded competition as an important and effective way of motivating children it was not over-stressed and the general approach was suitable and well-balanced.

7.142 In about half of the schools, pupils were encouraged to observe and to comment upon good practice in games, gymnastics or swimming, and in two-fifths of the schools, children were achieving a reasonable degree of manipulative skill, shown most clearly in games. Except for games which required pupils to react to changes as they arose in the course of play, much of the work in physical education was teacher-directed. In a small number of schools, pupils responded particularly well when making decisions in response to gymnastic tasks or problems ; in a few schools, they were encouraged to make decisions on the siting of apparatus, the selection of good examples of work and the organisation and refereeing of tournaments. In many schools, more opportunities need to be provided for children to discuss good performances and make their own decisions in relation to tasks or problems.

7.143 Almost all the schools expected children to change into appropriate clothing for physical education and, where there were facilities, to shower after games. Half the schools had a conscious policy of promoting an awareness of factors influencing good health, and most taught the principles of safety as they related to the use of swimming baths and apparatus. Sometimes, provision did little to support teachers' efforts in this respect, as when floors were dusty, indoor areas were of limited size, or the maintenance of equipment and playing surfaces was neglected.

7.144 Almost every school had a scheme of work for physical education as a separate subject, though schemes were used effectively in only one-third of the sample. Games and gymnastics received most attention, whereas dance was given detailed coverage in less than a quarter of schemes. About half the schemes adequately covered content and made reference to skill development, methodology and organisation. Ten covered progression in detail, and twice that number paid some regard to it. Safety and resources were adequately considered in only a few schemes.

7.145 Physical education was of a satisfactory standard in about three-fifths of the schools, although in some of these good work was achieved only in certain aspects of the subject. Tasks were set at an appropriate level of difficulty for the large number of children of average ability in three-fifths of the schools. Children who were less able at physical education were given suitable work in only half the sample, and the more able were provided with challenging activities in only two-fifths of the schools.

HEALTH EDUCATION

7.146 Aspects of health education figured in the curriculum of almost every school in the survey, in some cases as a separately timetabled subject but more often as a contributory element in other subjects such as physical education, home studies and religious education. Many of the schools visited were doing much to promote that part of health education which is concerned with encouraging good personal relationships through developing children's self-confidence and sense of personal responsibility.

7.147 Children need to understand how the body functions and what factors influence their health, growth and development. Elements of human biology were taught in over four-fifths of the schools visited ; much of this work was concentrated in the third and fourth years. In general, it was taught as part of the science curriculum, though home studies and physical education also made contributions to such topics as nutrition and the digestive and skeletal systems. In some cases, work consisted of copying detailed notes containing technical terms which were not adequately understood by the children. In a few classes, a practical approach to work on the five senses helped children to understand and appreciate the functioning of their bodies.

7.148 The physical changes associated with puberty were discussed in the majority of schools ; in about a fifth of the schools, boys and girls were taught separately for this topic. About half the schools consulted parents about sex education either by letter or by holding meetings at which the school's policy was explained. It was common practice for talks to be given to girls on menstruation and personal hygiene by teachers or by visiting nurses. Discussion of the emotional changes accompanying adolescence was much less in evidence. In general, teachers were helping pupils understand the nature of the physical changes that were affecting them, but too few schools helped allay pupils' worries by emphasising sufficiently the wide age variation in the onset of puberty. It is important that work related to sex education should be developed in full consultation with parents, should be in context rather than treated in isolation and should refer to the physical and emotional changes occurring at puberty, the reasons for these changes and the normality of the wide variation in age at which such changes occur.

7.149 Most schools paid attention to personal, domestic and community hygiene, particularly in home studies lessons. Children had first-hand experience of hygiene in the preparation of food, and in some schools this was complemented by other work, which ranged from studies of public health in nineteenth-century Britain to the use of experiments to illustrate the importance of hygiene. Allied concerns of schools were the teaching of safe habits of working in laboratories, gymnasia and craft areas and the development of an awareness of safety through road safety talks, films and cycling proficiency tests.

7.150 In almost half the schools some reference was made to environmental and social hazards, though the treatment of these topics was often incidental. Pollution, litter and conservation were topics that featured in a number of school assemblies. In one class, a visit to the Farne Islands led to work on pollution and the effects of oil on sea birds, which the teacher demonstrated by pouring oil into a tank of water and showing pupils the effect on feathers dipped into the tank. Many current social issues were raised in discussion which followed broadcast programmes on health. In this context, some teachers used imaginative approaches to some of the more frequently publicised social hazards such as smoking, inappropriate diets and misuse of medicines. Much of the discussion on controversial social issues was confined to the oldest pupils. Such issues are best discussed as part of a wide curriculum, preferably with children throughout the middle years.

7.151 The day-to-day life of classroom and school provides many opportunities for incidental learning about inter-personal relationships. In only a quarter of the sample were such relationships specifically studied as part of the health education course. Work on families and friends was sometimes provided for younger children, and in one school there was a course concerned with 'How people treat each other'.

7.152 In the planning of their work in health education, schools can call on help from area health education officers and from local education authority advisers, some of who have convened working parties, produced reports and run courses in health education. Outside speakers, too, can make a valuable contribution, provided their contributions are incorporated as an integral part of courses and are used by teachers as bases for further work in class. Outside help was used in over three-fifths of the survey schools. Visits from the police were common practice and were seen as means of highlighting safety on roads, railways and canals, and helping prevent vandalism through fostering a sense of social responsibility and community interest. Health visitors and nurses gave talks to pupils in almost two-fifths of the schools. Other contributions were made by health education officers, doctors and dental officers. Only a small number of schools referred to discussions with area health education officers about the formulation of school policies. Some good examples of teaching by outside visitors were reported. In one school, for example, a dental health education officer had worked with first year children and, as a result, a display had been mounted in the local town exemplifying the range and quality of work which could be done with pupils of this age group in dental health education.

7.153 Many schools have only recently become aware of the need to provide work in health education either as a separate subject on the timetable or as a contributory element in other subjects. To help the development of health education a member of staff might be given responsibility for planning a programme and co-ordinating the work. Schemes of work were found in only about half the schools and ranged from brief check-lists of possible topics to detailed documents containing aims, topics arranged in sequence, and advice on resources and teaching methods. To implement schemes of work, the schools require a wide range of reference books, audio-visual resources and materials from curriculum development projects. In the survey, only a quarter of the schools had sufficient resources to support a range of work. In more than half the schools, television programmes and films were important elements in the health education curriculum but only some of the schools provided adequate time for follow-up discussion of these.

HISTORY, GEOGRAPHY AND RELIGIOUS EDUCATION

Timetable arrangements

7.154 On the timetable of some of the schools, history and geography, sometimes together with religious education, were combined in broad areas of the curriculum described variously as humanities, social studies, environmental studies, integrated studies, project and topic work. In others, history, geography and religious education were timetabled as separate subjects for children in some or all year groups.

7.155 Work in history and geography in whatever circumstances it appeared in the curriculum was inspected in all 48 schools, but religious education was inspected only in the 33 county and 7 voluntary-controlled schools. For convenience, the work that was observed is presented in this section under each of the three subject headings, but their use should not be taken to imply that schools should necessarily use these divisions in the construction of their timetables.

7.156 In just under half the schools, history and geography were taught as part of subject combinations to children in all year groups ; in a few schools, religious education was also included. Of the remaining schools, most grouped history and geography together for some pupils, particularly the younger ones ; in a few cases, religious education, science or English formed part of such combinations. For third year children history and geography were taught as separate subjects in about two-fifths of the sample, and for fourth-year pupils in about three-fifths. Religious education was timetabled separately for all children in about three-quarters of the schools inspected and as a part of larger subject groupings for all or some pupils in the remainder.

History

7.157 History was taught in every school in the survey, in the majority of cases as a separate subject for the oldest pupils and as part of larger subject combinations for the remaining age groups. Where it was combined with other subjects in a humanities scheme the amount of time it received depended on the emphasis given to it by individual teachers. Where this was less than forty minutes per week, as in some schools, the time allocated was considered inadequate.

7.158 History was usually taught to mixed-ability classes. Normally, pupils worked either as whole classes or as individuals ; only a few schools used cooperative work in small groups or 'lead' lessons where particular topics were introduced to children from more than one class. A number of interesting lead lessons were seen. In one, the teacher used question-and-answer techniques, dialogue with another teacher and an audio-visual display to stimulate discussion about a town of historic interest. In another, a third-year class illustrated a teacher's lead lesson by playing snatches of the children's games she described and then going on to perform a previously rehearsed mummer's play for the pupils who were present from other classes.

7.159 Pupils studied aspects of English history in every school. Certain topics in world history such as ancient civilisations and voyages of discovery were very commonly taught, but elements of modern world history were under-emphasised in many schools. Local history was given the least emphasis but when taught it was often taught well and provided children with an appreciation of chronology which helped them place more distant events in context. Often, visits to local sites or museums were an integral part of such study. Activities included the examination of documents such as tax returns or census figures, the interviewing of local inhabitants and the examination and discussion of artefacts borrowed from local museums and other sources. The work done in some of the schools to foster children's understanding of the development of their localities demonstrated the value of the local environment as a source of first-hand experience and historical evidence, as a stimulus to children's enquiries and, for many, as a means of understanding their own roots.

7.160 In the schools more attention needs to be given to developing children's understanding of chronology and their appreciation of how and why change has taken place. In about half of the sample, pupils were developing an understanding of chronology by placing people, artefacts and events in time and arranging them in sequence in relation to one another and to other material previously studied. A similar proportion of schools were helping children develop an appreciation of change and continuity by getting them to consider basic questions of similarity and difference between different historical periods, and by encouraging them to examine the process of change in relation to the study of particular topics. One school, for example, fostered children's understanding of change through discussing how the poor were treated in Elizabethan, Victorian and modern England and encouraging the pupils to speculate on the causes of poverty. Other schools pursued lines of enquiry in relation to topics such as medicine, roads and entertainment. In only just over a third of the schools were children helped towards an understanding of causation and historical explanation by being required to consider people's motives in behaving as they did or by being asked how certain events and developments were inter-connected.

7.161 Nearly all the schools arranged visits to museums and historic sites to help children appreciate the conditions under which people lived at different times. This process was further fostered in just under half the schools, through imaginative writing such as 'eye-witness' accounts of such events as Viking invasions or diaries kept at the time of the Great Fire of London. Drama was occasionally used to encourage imaginative understanding, as when a group of children took the parts of Peruvian peasants airing their grievances in front of the district governor, or when a number of boys took it in turn to be William the Conqueror putting forward their claims for the English throne to their classmates. In a few schools, historical fiction was used as means of helping children to understand the feelings and problems of others : for example, a reading of an extract from *The Eagle of the Ninth* provided one class with an imaginative account of Roman gladiatorial combat.

7.162 The ability to use evidence in building up accounts and arguments is essential to an understanding of history. Primary source materials were used in less than half the schools, but some examples of good practice were seen. In one first year class, a probationary teacher made effective use of flints and

107

flint tools which she borrowed from the local museum and which she complemented with her own photographs of the Skara Brae excavations. However, in only a few classes were children helped sufficiently to locate, select and record information from different primary and secondary sources. In one project on the Victorian period, children made reference to a wide range of books, to well produced work sheets and wall charts, to artefacts and to photostats of contemporary newspaper articles. They used more than one source to answer questions, were encouraged to speculate on why certain things occurred and analysed and selected materials through group discussion. However in many more of the schools, children need to learn to identify, assess and use a variety of forms of evidence from primary sources such as artefacts, buildings and parish registers and from secondary sources such as an appropriate range of textbooks, film strips and reference books.

7.163 Although much of the children's work was illustrated, in only a minority of schools was pupils' historical understanding advanced by their accurate production of pictorial work based on careful observation. Three-dimensional work to promote historical learning was occasionally found ; for example, in the project mentioned previously some children made toys as part of their work on Victorian entertainment. Games were occasionally used, as in the school where pupils had learned much about the Napoleonic Wars through making, positioning and playing with models. More use could be made of games, simulations, fiction and classroom drama to help children enter imaginatively into the experience of others.

7.164 Pupils' response to the limited range of writing tasks set was considered satisfactory or better in two-thirds of the schools, as was the quality of their participation in oral work. In one school, for example, children discussed the pros and cons of emigration from Ireland at the time of the Potato Famine, while in another, pupils discussed the evidence they gained from interviewing local inhabitants about the history of their houses. Such discussions were exploratory and speculative though in too many cases a high proportion of oral exchange consisted of questions requiring brief answers. Children's satisfactory response to written and oral work suggested that there would be advantage in encouraging them more often to speculate and put forward arguments about motives, causes and effects.

7.165 Most schools had schemes of work for history, usually as part of a combined humanities course, but occasionally as a separate subject. Most of these placed considerable emphasis on content. About half included some reference to skills ; rather less than that mentioned ideas to be acquired by pupils. Very few paid attention to progression and the best means of achieving this. Where history was combined with other subjects, the close identification, in the schemes and subsequently by the teachers, of procedures particular to the subject was generally associated with successful learning, both in terms of knowledge and principles.

7.166 Standards of work in history were satisfactory in about half of the schools, including a small number where they were good. The considerable number of children of average ability were adequately provided for in half the sample, but less able pupils were given tasks at an appropriate level of difficulty in just over a third. Abler pupils were given work commensurate with their abilities in just over a quarter of the schools.

7.167 Whatever the arrangements made for the teaching of history, it is important that children do not see history as an isolated subject. They need to be introduced to the particular contribution history can make to understanding the past and the present but they also need to be aware of the historical dimension to other subjects such as art, science or religious education. For some aspects of the work, it might be appropriate to teach history separately for a time ; for other aspects, it might be appropriate to use a number of subjects in combination. The way work is organised should allow history to make its contribution either separately or in combination depending on the material being studied.

Geography

7.168 Geography was taught to all year groups in every school in the survey, often as a separate subject in the fourth year and as part of larger subject combinations in the first, second and third years. Standards of work were fair in about a third of the schools. Work of appropriate difficulty was given to the large proportion of pupils of average ability in about a third of the schools. In a similar proportion of schools, though not necessarily the same schools in each case, the needs of the more able and less able pupils were each being satisfactorily met.

7.169 In two-thirds of the schools, children in all year groups were taught geography in mixed-ability classes ; in the remaining third, some pupils, usually the older ones, worked in classes grouped according to ability. First and second year children were often taught geography by their class-teachers ; older pupils were more frequently taken by teachers who spent a substantial proportion of their time teaching geography. Children usually worked as individuals or as whole classes, but in about half the schools, opportunities were sometimes provided for children to work in small groups. In a few schools, cooperative teaching took place, occasionally involving lead lessons.

7.170 Most work in geography was closely directed by teachers. Children had a few opportunities to take responsibility for the planning and execution of their own work, but in a number of schools they were able to exercise initiative to some degree, for example, in the design and construction of instruments for weather recording, or in the display of their own photographs following field trips. In about two-thirds of the schools, children at some stage of the course were given work which required them to observe carefully. In the majority of these schools, pupils worked satisfactorily and in some, produced very accurate drawings, maps and models. In only about half the sample were children asked to record information which they had collected personally ; some pupils collected information from a variety of sources, collated it well, used it to make comparisons and recorded it in writing, maps, graphs and, sometimes photographs. In just over a third of the sample, some of the children were encouraged to select evidence relevant to the enquiry being pursued ; good work resulted in eight of the schools. In only a quarter of the schools, did pupils have to apply their geographical knowledge to other situations, for example to apply their understanding of how climate affects farming in Britain in order to speculate on such effects elsewhere.

7.171 Children in over two-thirds of the schools studied aspects of the environment at first-hand. Much use was made of the locality but visits were also made to more distant urban and rural locations, and two-fifths of the schools provide valuable opportunities for pupils to participate in residential fieldwork at least once, and often more, during their middle school career. Work outside school was frequently well prepared and followed-up but was sometimes limited to experiences involving observation and description with insufficient discussion of geographical ideas. In work on the environment, children need not only to be taught to observe carefully but also to seek explanations and to select evidence relevant to their enquiries. They should be encouraged and helped not only to describe places, features and activities, but also to investigate the significance of locations and distribution patterns and the relationships between people and their environment.

7.172 In the schools visited, themes were illustrated most frequently by reference to the locality or to the United Kingdom. Not many programmes of work used examples from the remainder of the Western World and the Developing World, and very few included aspects of the geography of communist countries. Farming and settlement were studied in every school ; in one-third of the sample, aspects of such themes were included for children in each year group. Industry, transport and land forms were considered rather less frequently, but were included in the geography course at some stage in all but a small number of schools. Natural resources did not feature as a theme in programmes of work of ten schools but were included for two or more age groups in almost half the sample. In some schools, more attention needs to be given to the range of places and themes which are selected for geographical study.

7.173 Reference was sometimes made to environmental and social problems in work on resources, population and pollution or on the siting of features such as power stations and airports, but very often the references were incidental rather than central to the work. In over half the schools, environmental and social problems were dealt with superficially or not at all ; more explicit attention to them would help children appreciate the relevance of such issues to the places they are studying.

7.174 In about half the schools, adequate attention was given to increasing pupils' knowledge of what places are like. Often, work on local areas was sound and field-work valuably complemented class work. In those schools where pupils' knowledge of places was good, case studies, local visits, class discussion and a variety of teaching aids were characteristic of the work. In one school, for example, work on the local district with second year pupils involved a visit, talks by outside speakers, the design and completion of questionnaires, the showing of films, the preparation of a tape-slide sequence and the forging of links with work in science.

7.175 Just over half the schools introduced children to how people have used and adapted their surrounding for various purposes. In a quarter, this was an important aspect of the course ; good work was based on carefully chosen case studies providing good second-hand experience and on local studies demonstrating man's changing influence. One school had a course specifically based upon old maps of the locality and the evidence these provided of changes over time. A quarter of the schools dealt with the general theme irregularly and at a descriptive level. In the remainder the use and adaptation of surroundings were given little attention, though occasional incidental references were made to them.

7.176 In over a quarter of the schools, pupils were developing a good understanding of the location of places, features and activities. In these schools, they were encouraged not only to identify and describe places but to

111

seek explanations for the location of features being studied. Class discussion, local fieldwork and the regular use of atlases and maps of different scales were important aspects of the work. In the remainder, although some work on location was done, children were not often helped to generalise about distributions ; even in the schools where examples of good practice were seen, these were often limited to the work of a few classes. In these classes recurring relationships had been clearly discussed with pupils and emphasised in such a way that children developed the ability to look for such relationships for themselves.

7.177 In many schools, more emphasis needs to be given to developing children's understanding of the links between places through the study of the movements of people and goods, and to developing their understanding of how and why changes take place in the location of activities and the character of places. Topic work sometimes provided opportunities for such work but activities often showed a historical bias and geographical aspects tended to be neglected.

7.178 Children consulted atlases as sources of information in almost all the schools, including six where they used atlases freely and confidently for a variety of purposes. In many schools, however, atlases were either restricted to particular classes or, although available to all, were used irregularly. Although the skills of using indexes and finding locations were often well practised and understood, little attention was given to helping children identify patterns, draw out relationships or seek explanations with the use of atlases. In almost half the schools, much work was done on the interpretation of Ordnance Survey maps, and simple exercises involving the interpretation of symbols were usually well done. Work with large-scale maps could often be extended so that pupils are helped to relate features shown on such maps to features in the environment and, as with atlases, to identify and interpret patterns. Globes could be used much more frequently in geography lessons. In only four schools were they used regulariy by children in different year grouups as part of work on location, latitude and longitude, and on the distortions involved in making flat maps of the world.

7.179 In two-thirds of the schools, children drew maps to record and convey information, but except in a small number, there was no clear understanding of how mapping could be developed. In many schools, mapping was not given adequate emphasis and reliance was placed on copying maps and on labelling and making additions to poor reproductions. Using maps to calculate distances was practised satisfactorily in less than a quarter of the schools, usually by older pupils. In some cases, especially when based on local work, the activity generated good discussion and provided opportunities for pupils to make estimates and judgements. Generally, more consideration needs to be given to developing pupils' skills in making their own maps.

7.180 Geography was usually taught in class bases. Specialist rooms which had storage provision and facilities for displays of materials specific to geography were found in fewer than two-fifths of the schools and were largely, but not exclusively, used by older pupils. In general, the accommodation was adequate for practical work and the use of maps, though some rooms lacked blackout facilities.

7.181 Just under half the sample had stocks of geography books which were satisfactory in both quantity and quality for the work being undertaken. In some schools, map work was hampered by the lack of adequate sets of atlases, and in some, reference books and materials were insufficient to support individual and group work. Many of the schools with less than adequate book supplies relied heavily on teacher-produced materials such as worksheets or information booklets, but only in a small number of cases were they satisfactory in terms of presentation, language and level. In general, schools were adequately provided with audio-visual equipment which was well used in over a quarter of the sample. Wall maps and charts were found in many schools and often used to good effect. Resources for geography teaching were usually dispersed and sometimes inadequately catalogued ; such resources were organised efficiently in only about a quarter of the schools.

7.182 Almost all the schools had schemes of work for geography, more frequently as part of combined schemes than as a separate subject. These had been compiled by those with responsibility for these subjects, usually in conjunction with heads or year group co-ordinators. Some made use of LEA guidelines for humanities where these had been provided. Most of the schemes provided general guidelines on content ; almost all needed amplification. In many cases, resources were referred to, either in the schemes themselves or in separate catalogues. Map skills were set out in almost a third of the schemes and skills used in reference work in rather more. However, very few schemes paid much attention to important ideas and underlying principles in geography or provided adequate guidance on how the work might be planned to achieve progression in learning. Work with older pupils more closely followed the schemes than work with younger ones ; where schemes were more closely followed, rather more examples of good work resulted.

7.183 Geography may be taught as a separate subject or as part of a broad area of the curriculum. Whatever timetable arrangements are made, it is important that there should be progression in the geographical skills and ideas taught during the four year course and that where appropriate, work in geography should be linked to other subjects such as history or religious education.

Religious education

7.184 Religious education was part of the curriculum in each of the forty county and voluntary controlled schools inspected. It was more often timetabled as a separate subject than as part of a larger combination. In about three-quarters of the schools, religious education was taught to children in mixed-ability classes ; within such classes, similar assignments were usually given to all pupils, although most teachers expected children of differing abilities to work at different levels and pace. In the remaining quarter religious education followed patterns of streaming or banding provided for humanities subjects. In most schools, the subject was timetabled for one or two periods per week, but in some cases, the time allocated was not always used for religious education. A few schools arranged religious education in blocks of lessons centred on topics which were spread through the year : this was usually done where a combined studies course involving religious education, history and geography had been developed. There were cases where, for pupils in some year groups, religious education was only provided in assemblies. A number of the schools need to consider whether more time should be allocated to the subject as a necessary step towards providing children with a full and suitably demanding course.

7.185 Many of the schools set a high value on assemblies and these were making a sensitive contribution to children's social and personal development, as well as making a specific contribution to their religious education, by fostering sympathy, tolerance and consideration for others. Various forms of assembly took place, often within the same school : whole school, year group, house or class assemblies were all reported. This variation was sometimes necessary because of the inadequate size of school halls but was sometimes employed to foster greater staff and pupil partici-pation in the life of the school. Assemblies for the whole school or for smaller groups were regularly taken by heads, deputy heads, year group co-ordinators and teachers responsible for 'houses'. Visiting ministers and clergy took assembly on a regular basis in a fifth of the schools. Usually children experienced some elements of traditional corporate worship such as hymns (often with modern tunes and words), prayers and scripture readings. A few schools considered material from other religious traditions and the occasional school reflected the festivals of other faiths, such as Divali. Often the ideas presented in assemblies were clearly intended to contribute to children's social and personal development and in many, there was a strong element of moral education. In three-quarters of the schools children contributed to assemblies through drama, mime, readings, prayers, choral work and orchestral music. Many of these contributions were the result of careful thought and planning by teachers and children, usually on a class basis. This often provided material for discussion in class. In most of these schools, pupils appeared to enjoy assembly, participated fully and responded well to the themes and ideas presented. In a few schools, where children were expected to be largely passive, they were sometimes restless or inattentive.

7.186 In five-sixths of the schools, the Bible was an important focus for work in class, but its background was not adequately considered in about half the sample. The life of Jesus was the most common topic taken from the New Testament, although about a quarter of the schools also included some study of the early Church for older pupils. Some schools used themes such as 'heroes', 'parables', or 'miracles' as a way of organising New Testament material for teaching purposes. In a number of schools, teachers succeeded in setting biblical material against the contemporary background. In one, the class acted out a Jewish school of the time, with the teacher as rabbi and children appropriately dressed with head-dresses, skull caps, prayer shawls and phylacteries. As a result of the teacher's skilful exposition and questioning, the children began to appreciate the religious significance of the objects they were wearing. In most schools, younger children heard some of the more vivid stories from the Old Testament, but these were not often developed later in the course to ensure that pupils understood something of the nature and religious significance of such stories. In about three-quarters of the schools, Old Testament material was not considered by third and fourth year pupils, although in others, some such material was included as part of themes such as 'rules of life' or 'sacred places'. Some schools failed to introduce a sufficiently wide range of Biblical material, especially for older children, or to give attention to the different kinds of writing in the Bible or to discuss the historical and geographical settings of biblical stories.

7.187 Just under half the schools discussed the lives of famous Christians, and some examined the festivals of the Church, occasionally together with the festivals of other faiths. About a quarter of the schools gave some attention to the history of the Christian Church. In one of these, current events in Ireland led to a study of the Roman Catholic and Anglican churches and the religious history of Northern Ireland, and eventually to the consideration of the children's own religious traditions.

7.188 Religious education has an important part to play in an increasingly multi-faith and multi-cultural society. Just over half the schools inspected were attempting to inform children about world faiths other than Christianity, especially those represented in Britain today, but many schools lacked library books and other teaching resources to support this work. The extent of the work ranged from single lessons on particular faiths in some schools to, in one case, two-thirds of the religious education provided for fourth year pupils. Aspects of Islam, Buddhism, Hinduism, Sikhism, and Judaism were most usually discussed but were often treated as self-contained topics, unrelated to one another or to other areas of work. However, a small number of schools examined a range of religious activities and beliefs through such themes as 'symbols', 'sacred writings' and 'festivals'. In one school the work was planned carefully from the first to the fourth year to cover such themes and also to give separate consideration to Judaism, Islam, Hinduism, and Buddhism. Work in history and geography occasionally included reference to world religions. Some schools were also responding in other ways to the multi-cultural nature of their catchment area ; visits were arranged to places of worship, visitors from various faiths were invited to discuss their beliefs and practices, and children were encouraged in class to make their contributions, such as a Hindu boy describing festivals of his own religion.

7.189 Although some individual teachers gave attention to myths, legends and parables in English lessons, few schools helped pupils to understand the character of religious language, or to appreciate the significance of myth, symbolism and ritual. There was effective work in one school where the study of Greek myths, the creation stories and the patriarchal sagas was followed by work on religious symbols such as the Cross and the Star of David which led to visits to the local church and synagogue to highlight the significance of ritual and worship.

7.190 In about half the schools, classes were observed discussing important religious issues such as 'good and evil', 'suffering and death', 'creation' and 'vocation'. In some cases, discussion of these topics had been planned by teachers and in others, it arose incidentally from Bible stories, social issues, local events, biographies and other starting points. At times, however, there was a failure to respond to the interest and concern shown by pupils in such matters, because teachers felt they were peripheral to the work in hand. Many religious ideas are difficult to understand and talk about but teachers in the schools need to encourage children to discuss such issues.

7.191 Writing was a major activity in religious education lessons in most schools, but this was often to answer questions from text books, worksheets or the blackboard, or to reproduce in pupils' own words stories read or heard in class. Only occasionally were children encouraged to write from personal experience or to express a personal standpoint on issues raised in class. Occasionally good writing resulted from appropriate discussion and from reference to several sources in addition to the Bible or the text-book. In one school work on William Blake written as an English project produced sensitive writing on mysticism and imagery. One child wrote 'He seemed to me to have really wanted to understand human beings. . . . I think some of his poems make me feel a little sad but he must have been a very fine man who did or tried to understand human imagination and feelings, from fearsome utter anger to gentle happiness and harmony. If I could have met this man I am sure he would have been a great friend of mine.' In some schools, discussion was an important aspect of the work ; in some classes it was given high priority and conducted well. There were instances, however, where children had little opportunity to discuss the ideas presented, where their own questions such as "Why is Good Friday called 'good'?" and "Is there life after death?" were not pursued and where too much emphasis was placed on writing, sometimes perhaps as a means of avoiding such discussion. Teachers in a third of the schools made some use of drama in religious education lessons, often in preparation for class-led assemblies. Although the use of drama in normal class work was limited, examples of good practice were seen which led to pupils developing greater understanding of other people's attitudes. Pictorial work was largely confined to the illustration of children's writing by drawings and pictures which were often copied. The general lack of reference books and other visual media restricted the models available to pupils. Music was rarely used in lessons but was often strongly featured in assemblies and in school productions based on well-known religious themes and performed for parents and the local community.

7.192 As caring, considerate communities, the schools were fostering values and attitudes important in religious education. Good pastoral care, sensitively conducted assemblies and the example set by staff helped to create a climate where it was possible to consider the needs and feelings of others, including those who were disadvantaged, both within the school community and outside it. In one school a film about the work of Dr Barnardo had, in addition to producing money-raising ventures, generated discussions about suffering, neglected children and goodness. Appeals through the *Blue Peter* programme for help in devastated areas had similarly enlisted constructive sympathy and contributed towards a growing sense of the responsibility of individuals towards their immediate society and the world community. A third of the schools seemed successful in combining the developing of such favourable attitudes with some growth in children's understanding of the nature of personal faith and its effect on people's lives. But, in general, the children in the schools need to participate more actively in religious education. Assemblies, class activities such as drama, visits to places of religious significance and personal contributions through discussion, writing and work in art would serve to stimulate children's interest as well as to help them understand the significance of the matters with which religious education deals.

7.193 The schools need to improve their stocks of books and other teaching resources for religious education. In over half the schools inspected, the supply of books and audio-visual materials was inadequate and in only about half was the quality of such resources satisfactory. The books used were often class books and only occasionally were these supplemented by slides, film-strips or other audio-visual aids. However, in one school, all classes of older pupils read biographies, saw relevant film-strips, listened to tape-recordings and referred to an appropriate range of books.

7.194 Four-fifths of the schools made some use of resources available outside the school ; nearly half of them invited visitors to speak about local religious communities or charitable organisations. Visits to local churches and other places of worship were occasionally arranged as part of work in humanities, environmental studies or religious education. Visits to abbeys and cathedrals were sometimes made as part of day excursions or extended school journeys.

7.195 Three-quarters of the schools where religious education was inspected had schemes of work or guidelines for each year group. The remainder provided them for specific year-groups or, in a few cases, had no schemes. In the schools which had schemes of work these reflected to a varying degree the Agreed Syllabus adopted locally. Most schemes treated religious education as a separate subject rather than as part of a larger subject combination. Most placed considerable emphasis on content, which some listed under broad thematic headings. Topics such as 'caring' or 'courage' were typical of those selected for young children, and 'sacred places' or 'festivals' were characteristic of the more specifically religious themes suggested for older pupils. Some schemes did little more than list stories from the Bible and many failed to clarify the important religious ideas to be explored, the principles governing the selection of stories and the level at which the stories should be approached. Only a few schemes provided adequate guidance on progression, teaching methods and resources or referred to how material might be related to pupils' own experience. In a small number of schools, a good variety of work was fostered as a result of carefully devised schemes which discussed the ground to be covered, the religious ideas to be explored, the methods and the resources which could profitably be employed and the skills which should be developed by the work.

7.196 The general standard of work achieved by pupils in religious education was satisfactory or better in about two-fifths of the schools, including a small number where it was good overall. Assignments at a suitable level of difficulty were provided for the large number of pupils of average ability in almost half the sample. In each case, children of above average and below average were given appropriately challenging work in less than a quarter of the schools.

8 Some issues for discussion

Introduction

8.1 This report is based on a survey of the work observed in 48 9−13 middle schools during the school year 1979−80. The schools illustrated the diversity of circumstances in which 9−13 middle schools operated but did not constitute a statistically representative sample. The fall in the number of children of school age, which was already affecting 9−13 school intakes at the time of the survey, has continued. While it is not claimed that generalisations arising from the survey apply to all 9−13 middle schools in 1983, it is likely that many of the findings will be of interest to those concerned with 9−13 schools or indeed with the 9−13 age range or part of it. Although a diversity of practice was found in the survey schools, a number of broad issues emerged which may be of value to teachers, administrators, advisers, teacher trainers and governors. Some of these general issues do not apply to 9−13 middle schools alone but manifest themselves, although with some differences, in all schools. Some themes, such as the match between the training and the work of teachers or the viability of small middle schools, have come into greater prominence in professional discussion since the time of the survey as a result of government initiatives or because of the continuing effects of factors such as falling rolls.

Transition

8.2 The survey schools, like all middle schools, attempted to ensure that in the education they provided they achieved a transition from primary education, which their first-year intake had recently experienced, towards secondary education, to which their oldest pupils would transfer at a crucial time in their educational career. They would then be only a year away from option choices that would set the pattern of their subsequent qualifications.

The schools had to judge what was an appropriate curriculum ; how to match the demands made on children with their stage of development ; and how to achieve continuity of learning, both over the four-year span and in relation to children's learning in first and upper schools. The schools in the survey used a range of organisational devices and deployed staff in a variety of ways to move from an organisation based on one teacher to one class for most subjects in year one, to one based largely on the use of separate subject teachers in year four.[1] In most cases, such organisational arrangements provided a suitable transition though, as elsewhere, some schools found it difficult to provide effective continuity in children's learning,[2] or to achieve a satisfactory match between the demands made on children and their stage of development.[3]

Curricular policies

8.3 One significant step by which progress might be made in overcoming these widely recognised difficulties would be the formulation of overall curricular policies and greater attention to planning within areas of the curriculum. Indeed, a feature of many of the schools in the survey was the effort made to provide continuity, particularly in English, mathematics, science and French as pupils passed from their middle to their upper schools.[4] For these subjects it was common for middle and upper school staff to consult about ways to ensure greater continuity of experience for the pupils. When drawing up such curricular policies, and they should be the result of discussion between heads, teachers and governors, there would be profit in taking into account the broad guidance provided in the Department's publication, *The school curriculum*,[5] and points made in local education authority policy statements on the curriculum. The schools' policy statements need to embody their general educational intentions and to firmly establish appropriate expectations related to the wide range of pupils' abilities, aptitudes and educational needs in the age range 9 – 13. Moreover, because the middle school is, by definition, an intermediate stage in education, these curricular policies need to be related to those formulated in the schools to which and from which middle school children transfer. Changes in the curricula of upper schools consequent on reappraisals

---

[1] Paragraphs 2.3 and 3.15-3.18
[2] Paragraphs 2.17-2.18
[3] Paragraph 2.15
[4] Paragraphs 6.21-6.22
[5] *The school curriculum*, DES, 1981

following the Department's Circular 6—81 ;[1] initiatives such as the New Technical Vocational Education Initiative ; and developments in the public examinations system, may well have implications for the curricula of middle schools. Together with measures to increase parental choice these developments reinforce the need for heads and teachers in middle schools to consult with those in upper schools to provide curricular policies which increase the coherence and continuity in children's education.

Progression

8.4 To ensure continuity of learning – a necessary condition for progression – it is important that the work done in subjects or parts of the curriculum in each of the four year groups should be referred to, and built on, in subsequent years. Progression is easier to manage in those parts of the curriculum where activities can be ordered according to clear logical sequences, but it also needs to be sought in areas or subjects where it is not possible to be so precise. The need for adequate progression is more likely to be met where schemes of work provide guidance on the skills, ideas and understandings children are to acquire and on the standards to be aimed at at various stages of the course while making due allowance for individual abilities.[2] In addition, schemes need to make explicit both the increasing demands to be made on children as they progress through the school and the differences in approaches to learning which are to be introduced so that these demands are progressively met.

Continuity between schools

8.5 The general coordination of curricular policies outlined in paragraph 8.3 will be the more effective if accompanied by more specific dove-tailing of approaches in particular subjects between the middle schools as a group in any one local education authority and between them and the schools to which and from which their pupils transfer. Continuity of this kind is difficult to achieve. There was evidence from the survey,[3] of activities designed to promote closer liaison with other schools for the benefit of children about to transfer. In general, consultation over the curriculum did not appear to be as well established as procedures for familiarising children with the schools to

---

[1] *The school curriculum*, 6—81
[2] Paragraph 6.3
[3] Paragraphs 2.17-2.18, 6.16-6.19, 6.21-6.23

which they were about to transfer. It is important that agreement about what is to be taught should be sought among local groups of middle schools and with first as well as with upper schools, and that it should not be restricted to a small number of subjects or areas of the curriculum.

Range of work

8.6 An issue related to progression concerns the range of the work to be introduced to middle school children and the depth of treatment accorded to different subjects or topics. In the survey schools, judgements on this question varied, not only among schools but often from subject to subject within the same school. The issue takes a variety of forms. For example, is it better in arts and crafts to introduce pupils to a wide range of media or to select a smaller number and encourage children to develop a degree of mastery of these through deeper study and more extensive experience? Should, for example, work in history involve an extensive treatment of many developments over a long period of time, or should more intensive study be made of particular aspects of human affairs at particular times and places? In general, a balance seems desirable and needs to be kept in mind when work is being planned and results are being assessed. Though children ought to have a variety of experience within a subject, they also need to study some aspects in greater depth if they are to develop a fuller understanding of some of the key features in particular areas of study. Work in depth is particularly important for able pupils so that they can be challenged to extend their thinking and to apply what they have learned to the exploration or solution of increasingly complex problems.

Organisation of the curriculum

8.7 In 9 – 13 middle schools, there has been considerable discussion as to the extent to which subjects in the humanities and arts and crafts should be taught separately or in combination and how such treatment aids or hinders children in their learning. The findings of the survey,[1] suggest that neither form of organisation possesses over-riding advantages ; good standards of work can be achieved when subjects are taught separately or in combination. Whatever the chosen organisation children should be introduced to the particular contribution which a specific subject makes to increasing their understanding and they should be aware how skills and ideas developed in

---

[1] Paragraph 3.29

one subject can be applied to others. An important factor to be borne in mind when any decision is made about the organisation of the curriculum is how far the proposed organisation is compatible with present teachers' strengths, particularly the subjects or broad areas studied by them as main subjects in initial training courses.

Approaches to learning

8.8 The survey indicates that much of children's time in school is spent in listening and writing.[1] Not many opportunities are provided for extended discussion, for collaborative work in groups, or for the exercise of choice, responsibility and initiative within the curriculum. A greater diversity of teaching and learning approaches should be provided for children across the four-year span,[2] but especially for older pupils, as a means of enhancing motivation to learn and quality of work. In all schools the local environment provides an obvious, though often ignored, starting point for children's enquiries ; it is a rich focus for work which can involve children in observation, description, application of skills and ideas, and, increasingly as they grow older, explanation, reasoned argument and generalisation. An expansion in the range of learning approaches, coupled with an increase in the demands made on children as they develop, will provide more opportunities for all pupils, from the least to the most able, to acquire and develop levels of skills and an understanding of ideas more clearly related to their capacities than is often the case at present.

Recent developments

8.9 In planning and reviewing curricula, account always has to be taken of developments in society in general including those specific changes reflected in current national and local education policies. In particular, the multi-racial nature of British society and often of the pupils in the schools ought to find reflection in the programme of work in ways that recognise difference of life style but confirm and emphasise a common heritage. It is also important that consideration is given to such different issues as the growing concern over the quality of the environment, developments in the field of micro-computers, and work in craft, design and technology. There are important messages to be responded to in the Cockcroft Report,

---

[1] Paragraphs 2.9 and 7.11
[2] Paragraph 2.10

Mathematics counts,[1] and in the consultative papers on science education and modern languages published recently by the Department of Education and Science. The extent to which curricular priorities can be ordered and re-ordered by a school depends on the suitability of available resources and the way their balance can be adjusted to match new needs but relies in the main on the professional response of the teaching staff.

Differentiation

8.10 Typically 9–13 schools have to meet a wide range of learning needs ranging from those of children who experience difficulty in reading, writing and number to those of able pupils who show ability and attainment comparable to those of some school leavers. Within any year group, ability and attainment will vary quite dramatically. The year group may well include some children who, in the language of the Warnock Report,[2] and the 1981 Education Act, have special educational needs. Some of them may have difficulties which require specialised teaching techniques or specialised equipment if the impediments to their learning are to be minimised or removed. Providing appropriately for the full range of their pupils' learning needs is a formidable professional challenge facing the teachers in all types of schools. The survey[3] indicates that in 9–13 schools children of average abilities are best provided for, since work is most often planned and implemented with them in mind. Less able children are quite often given work to take account of their difficulties, but in many schools able pupils are often not challenged sufficiently. Demanding activities, such as the interpretation of evidence in history or geography, the independent writing of continuous text in French or the exploration of patterns leading to generalisation in mathematics, should be provided more frequently, particularly in the work given to older pupils. In general, objectives and approaches need to be more clearly differentiated within each year group to cater more effectively for the range of children's capabilities and from the first to the fourth year to help ensure that increasingly demanding tasks are provided as children develop.

Use of subject teachers

8.11 Almost all the schools used a combination of class and subject teachers and for the great majority of children the emphasis on subject teaching was

---

[1] *Mathematics counts*, DES, 1982
[2] *Special educational needs*, DES, 1978
[3] Paragraph 2.15

increased as they moved up through the school. The findings of the survey,[1] revealed an association between higher overall standards of work and those schools with a greater use of subject teachers, an arrangement which occurred mainly in the third and fourth years. In seven schools substantial use of subject teachers was introduced into second-year classes. Five of these were among the schools which achieved significantly higher standards of work. These findings suggest that the learning needs of most, though not necessarily all, second year children might best be met by more use of subject teachers in a number of areas of the curriculum without at the same time destroying the close association children enjoy with their class teacher for a substantial part of their work.

Size of schools

8.12 The fall in the number of children of school age is likely to lead to smaller middle schools. With less than three forms of entry, 9–13 middle schools are unlikely to be able to provide the range of specialist teaching required to cover the curriculum and to cater adequately for all their pupils, unless their staffing ratios are considerably better than the average (20:1 in January 1983) for all such schools. This view was embodied in the Department's Circular (2/81) on falling rolls,[2] and evidence from the survey supports it ; the standards of work achieved in schools larger than three-form entry, in particular those of four-form entry, were generally higher than those achieved in schools smaller than three-form entry, although the latter had, on average, more favourable pupil/teacher ratios.[3] Where rolls are falling, the choice would seem to be between staffing disproportionately those 9–13 middle schools with less than three forms of entry, or closing or amalgamating them to form larger schools.

Staff levels and deployment of teachers

8.13 Even in schools with more than three forms of entry, the provision of the right mix of class and subject teachers for the school as a whole makes heavy demands on staffing within overall pupil/teacher ratios often less favourable than those provided in secondary schools. As a result, in schools of all sizes the present overall level of staffing leaves little margin of teacher-time for

---

[1] Paragraph 3.19 and Appendix 2 Paragraphs 3, 7 and 8
[2] Circular 2–81, *Falling rolls and surplus places*
[3] Appendix 2 : footnote to Paragraph 7

purposes other than the teaching of a class. The survey,[1] suggests that the tight level of staffing shows particularly in the work load of two groups of teachers : those who hold both organisational and curricular responsibilities and those who have oversight of two subjects or areas of the curriculum. While it is reasonable to expect such teachers to give some personal time to planning work, managing resources, and keeping up-to-date with developments, they also need sufficient opportunities while the schools are in session, to observe the work the children are doing and to guide and support other teachers. A very heavy teaching load inevitably limits their effectiveness as consultants or coordinators. This is an issue that deserves further study by those who determine teacher supply and staffing levels for middle schools. Although in most cases their room for manoeuvre is limited, schools too need to consider the problem ; they might, with benefit, re-examine the way teachers are deployed, the size of teaching groups, and the allocation of non-teaching time to see whether more time can be made available to help teachers discharge curricular and organisational responsibilities more effectively.

Teachers with special responsibilities

8.14 Consideration also needs to be given to other ways of increasing the standing and the effectiveness of teachers with special curricular responsibilities so that they can play an influential part in tackling the general curricular issues discussed earlier in this chapter and the more particular subject-related issues raised in Chapter 7. In many schools, stronger coordination throughout the four year span by teachers is required to provide appropriate progression in the work. In a large number of schools, the duties of year group coordinators and those of teachers with curricular responsibilities could usefully be spelled out, and the complementary nature of their respective roles clarified.

Teachers' initial qualifications

8.15 The White Paper, *Teaching quality*,[2] drew attention to the lack of fit between some teachers' initial qualifications and their tasks. It reported that the expertise of primary teachers now in service is heavily weighted towards the humanities and aesthetic subjects ; and it referred to evidence from HM

---

[1] Paragraphs 3.8-3.9
[2] *Teaching quality*, Cmnd 8836, 1983

Inspectors' survey of secondary education,[1] of 'insufficient match in many schools between the qualifications and experience of teachers and the work they are undertaking'. Judging from the findings of the present survey,[2] both observations apply, albeit with some modifications, to 9—13 middle schools. This is not surprising since in general 9—13 middle schools have teachers with a wide variety of training backgrounds, and deliberately employ a 'mixed economy' of class and subject teaching which, within current staffing limits, leads to teachers teaching several subjects to children in one or more year groups. Lack of fit between the teachers' main subjects studied in initial training and their subsequent teaching tasks is sometimes exacerbated as rolls fall by the loss of teachers with specific expertise who are not replaced.

8.16 The White Paper recognised that progress in improving fit can only be gradual. Nevertheless, middle schools might aid this process by reviewing their current patterns of staff deployment to make optimum use of the teaching expertise available, and those responsible for appointing teachers by considering even more carefully the initial training and qualifications of applicants for new posts. As the White Paper's recommendations on the content of initial training take effect, middle schools should be able to appoint newly qualified and trained teachers whose expertise can then be matched more effectively than at present to the tasks they have to perform in schools.

8.17 Both primary and the secondary courses of initial training operating in accordance with the White Paper's proposals will have to be able to equip student teachers with the knowledge and skills required to make an effective contribution to the education of children in 9—13 middle schools. The evidence of the survey suggests that the balance of the subject specialist to generalist should be such that there are some specialist subject teachers available for the second and the third years of the 9—13 school and that teaching by subject specialists for nearly all subjects in the fourth year would be a desirable aim. Consideration also needs to be given to the role of the subject specialist as consultant — available to all teachers, but particularly with time to work alongside the generalist class teacher as occasion demands.

In-Service training and support

8.18 Middle school teachers, as teachers elsewhere, need not only appropriate initial training but also opportunities for relevant in-service training. Staff development within individual schools is of particular

---

[1] *Aspects of secondary education in England*, DES, 1979
[2] Paragraphs 2.20 — 2.22, 3.13 — 3.14 and Appendix I, Paragraph 7

importance. Heads, deputy heads and teachers with curricular responsibilities can play an important part in this process through, for example, staff meetings to evaluate current practices, discussion with colleagues individually, joint production of resources, collaborative planning of schemes or programmes of work, or, where staffing levels allow, working alongside teachers in class. In addition, in-service training provision by local education authority advisers and other agencies is needed, including that relevant to the recent developments and initiatives identified in paragraph 8.9. Given the mix of generalist and specialist staffing found in the survey schools and the finding that most teachers teach across a range of subjects, in-service training that helps to improve teachers' subject competence will continue to be of particular importance to 9–13 middle schools. Curricular planning and organisation and the parts played by year group coordinators and curricular consultants are also appropriate topics for consideration in in-service training courses.

Contact with the two-tier system

8.19 A number of local education authorities maintain both two-tier and three-tier systems ; in these areas and in the broad national context, there would be mutual advantage in closer contact between the schools in the two systems. For example, in-service courses which examine ways in which work may be planned and organised to provide appropriately for children of varying abilities in the age range 9–13 years, regardless of the type of school attended, could benefit teachers in both two- and three-tier systems and lessen the feeling of isolation sometimes felt by teachers in areas where middle schools are a minority provision.

Conclusion

8.20 The middle schools reported on in this survey revealed many of the same strengths and weaknesses found in inspections of primary and secondary schools. Like most schools everywhere they have had to face and cope with the consequences of falling numbers and financial constraint. But unlike primary and secondary schools they have the task of providing for their pupils a gradual, phased transition from primary to secondary schooling. Such a phased transition has real and potential benefit for all pupils and some of the schools in this survey are achieving a fair degree of success in bringing it about. However, being an intermediate stage between two different modes of schooling makes particular demands upon both the providers and the practitioners : the LEAs and the teachers. For example, the mixture of generalist and specialist accommodation and the balance and mix of the teaching staff must be such as to enable the schools to offer an education that, within the one school, moves from the organic whole of class teaching to the introduction and establishment of specialist subject teaching across the range of the secondary curriculum, though not necessarily requiring a specialist subject teacher for every subject for pupils of first year secondary age.

8.21 When middle schools were established in the 1960s, the choice of 9 – 13 middle schools was based on a number of assumptions about stability in educational provision and demand that have not been borne out with the passage of time. Even in the 1960s carrying out this intermediate role placed relatively heavy demands upon those providing the human and material resources and upon the heads and teachers responsible for the organisation of teaching and learning in the schools. At a time of falling rolls and financial constraint the difficulties inherent in being 'in the middle' are exacerbated. For example, in 9 – 13 middle schools of less than four-form entry, as in small schools generally, if they are not disproportionately staffed, the quality of the education offered will suffer. If they are so staffed, the costs per pupil offered may be higher than those of providing equivalent education for the 9 – 13 age range in separate primary and secondary schools. More particularly the subject sections of this report reveal deficiencies in specialist accommodation and facilities, uncertainty that even for the oldest pupils all subjects can or will be covered by subject specialists and too much teaching that is aimed at the average level of ability. None of these factors is peculiar to middle schools but they appear to be related, in part at least, to the relatively high cost of meeting the need both for the generalist teachers that may be required for the primary phase and for specialist teachers which are required for the secondary phase.

8.22 The links revealed in this report between a higher incidence of subject teaching and higher standards of work in those subjects have implications not only for middle schools but also for the top two years of primary education. These findings raise again long-standing questions about the age at which children should be introduced to subject teaching, how and when the balance between generalist and specialist teaching should change and the age of transfer from primary to secondary education. These are large and far-reaching questions, but if 9 – 13 middle schools are to continue to provide a transition from primary to secondary modes, as originally envisaged, and to perform, age for age, as well as primary and secondary schools are expected to perform, given the present and likely trend of falling rolls, they will become increasingly expensive. It may be that this is a price worth paying for a form of schooling that emerged from careful consideration of the educational needs of children in this age range. But some of the practical difficulties facing 9 – 13 middle schools have been revealed in this survey and, in the present economic circumstances, carrying the relatively higher costs of middle schools sharply decreasing in size will have consequences elsewhere in the system. Moreover, the findings about relationships between size of school, subject teaching and higher standards of work, raise questions about the provision of effective and efficient education for 9 – 13 year olds that go beyond the particular issue of middle schools themselves.

Appendix 1   Background to the schools

INTRODUCTION

1. The illustrative sample of schools used in the survey was drawn from schools in 28 local education authorities. The sample comprised 33 maintained schools, 7 voluntary-controlled schools, 7 voluntary-aided schools and 1 special agreement school. One local education authority had 6 schools in the sample ; another had 4. Three local education authorities each had 3 schools in the sample, and the remaining 23 authorities each had 1 or 2 schools. Some of the schools were in local education authorities where 9 – 13 schools provided for a minority of pupils in the age-range 9 to 13.

2. The schools were selected to cover a range of size and catchment areas, to include schools housed in ex-primary, ex-secondary and purpose-built premises and to include schools transferring pupils to one or to a considerable number of upper schools. The resulting sample of 50 schools was weighted towards smaller schools and towards those which were purpose-built, in order to represent sufficiently these categories of schools. The size of the survey schools varied considerably, from large schools with over 600 pupils on roll to small schools with fewer than 150 children. All but two schools were co-educational and all had been open for four or more years with the 9 – 13 age-range only.

3. The catchment areas from which the middle schools drew their pupils were predominantly rural in 11 cases, predominantly urban in 26 and mixed in the remainder. Six of the schools had been designated as Social Priority Area schools and a few others were in areas with marked social difficulties. The number of first schools from which the middle schools received pupils varied from 1 to 21 ; the number of upper schools to which middle school pupils transferred varied from 1 to 12.

TEACHERS AND OTHER STAFF

4. Most teachers in the middle schools were employed as full-time members of staff. Of the remainder, some were part-time and others were peripatetic or visiting teachers who taught in a number of schools. In the survey schools, there were 1,003 teachers[1] of whom 94 per cent were employed full-time. 57 per cent of the teachers were women. Of the 48 heads, 5 were women.

5. As Table 15 shows, about a quarter of the teachers had taken first degrees and of these, just under half had Bachelor of Education degrees. Because of the move towards an all-graduate profession which involved the introduction of the Bachelor of Education degree and the phasing out of the Certificate in Education, graduate status was more common among more recently qualified teachers : 63 per cent of those who had been teaching for one year or less had taken degrees before becoming teachers compared with 12 per cent of those who had been teaching for more than ten years. Graduates were distributed evenly across the different size-bands of schools.

6. Partly because of the relatively recent introduction of middle schools, many teachers in the survey had not been trained specifically to teach in this type of school, although the training almost all had received for teaching children in primary or secondary schools covered all, or part, of the age-range in 9–13 schools. Some of the more recently trained teachers had taken middle-years courses, designed partly with middle schools in mind. In all, 42 per cent of the teachers in the sample had taken either junior-secondary or middle-years courses, 23 per cent had taken primary courses and 33 per cent had taken secondary courses[2]. Teachers who had been secondary-trained included about three-quarters of those teaching and qualified in home studies and a similar proportion of those teaching and qualified in craft, design and technology. About half of those teaching and qualified in physical education or in science had taken secondary courses of initial training. The phase-training backgrounds of teachers with special responsibilities are shown in Table 16.

7. The teachers in the survey studied one or more main subjects as part of courses leading to the award of first degrees or certificates in education. Table 17 shows the number of teachers who studied main subjects related to broad areas of the curriculum such as humanities and arts and crafts and to

---

[1] In this section, the term 'teachers', unless otherwise stated, refers to all teaching staff including heads but excluding peripatetic teachers.
[2] 2 per cent of teachers were graduates who had qualified teacher status but who had not taken initial training courses.

particular school subjects such as music or mathematics. The broad areas of arts and crafts, humanities, modern languages, English and physical education are sub-divided into constituent subjects in Table 18, which shows the number of teachers who had studied these subjects as main subjects in their initial training. During their initial training, most of the teachers also studied a range of professional courses designed to help them teach subjects or areas of the curriculum in addition to their main subjects.

8. In addition to initial qualifications, 15 per cent of all teachers had obtained further qualifications. Of these, about half had taken diplomas and a similar proportion had been awarded first or higher degrees.

9. As part of the background data collected from the schools, the heads were asked to indicate, in relation to a list of subjects and topics, how many teachers currently on their staff had attended various types of in-service training during the three years preceding the survey. In all, heads recorded over 2600 cases of teachers who had attended the types of courses specified.[1] Very many of the teachers had attended a number of courses. Table 19 shows how these cases of attendance were distributed over various types of course. The proportion of teachers from small schools taking in-service courses was similar to the proportion of teachers from other size- bands of schools ; there was no evidence that teachers from small schools were unable to get release for courses during school time. Teachers had taken part in courses on a wide range of areas and subjects, especially mathematics, language, reading and physical education, as well as courses on general aspects of the curriculum and organisation of middle schools. Many of these courses helped teachers to decide on the content of work to be covered and to identify the skills and concepts which the children should learn. The courses were particularly useful to teachers responsible for subjects other than those taken as main students in their initial training.

10. All the heads and almost all the deputies and senior teachers had been teaching for more than ten years. Almost all of those coordinating the work of year groups had had more than five years' teaching experience and most more than ten. Of those teachers with special curricular responsibilities, over four-fifths had taught for more than five years. Overall, 70 per cent of the

---

[1] This total underestimated the actual number of courses attended, as teachers who attended more than one course of a particular type and relating to the same subject were counted only once.

teachers had been teaching for more than five years.[1] Almost two-thirds of the teachers had been at the same middle school for four years or more ; about one-sixth had spent under a year in the school in which they were teaching, including 45 who were probationary teachers.

11. Teachers in schools are paid on a series of salary scales rising from Scale 1 to Scale 4 and beyond that to senior teacher, deputy head and head. The proportion of teachers on each scale in the 48 schools and in each of the size-bands of school is shown in Table 22. About one-third of the teachers in the survey were on Scale 2 and one in six on Scale 3. In each of the three size-bands, almost two-thirds of the teachers were paid on scales above Scale 1.

12. For each school in the survey, the overall pupil-teacher ratio was calculated by dividing the number of pupils on roll by the total teaching staff, including the head and part-time teachers[2] but excluding peripatetic teachers. In the sample as a whole, the pupil-teacher ratio ranged from 13.2:1 to 24.6:1. In general, the small schools had more favourable pupil-teacher ratios than the larger ones (see Table 23).

13. All but four of the schools had peripatetic or visiting teachers. In forty-two schools peripatetic teachers provided instrumental tuition ; the number of such staff varied from 1 peripatetic teacher in each of 5 schools to 5 or more teachers in 13 schools. The amount of tuition provided ranged from 2 hours or less a week in 5 schools to 15 hours or more in 6. In about a quarter of the sample peripatetic teachers were employed to help with remedial reading and, in a small number, to teach class music.

14. Each school in the sample had staff in addition to teaching staff. All had secretarial assistance and about half had ancillary staff who worked in libraries. Laboratory assistants were employed in about half of the schools, and in a minority ancillary help was provided for one or more of home studies,

---

[1] Details of the ages of the teachers and the length of their teaching experience are given in Tables 20 and 21.
[2] In calculating pupil-teacher ratios, part-time teachers were converted to the full-time equivalent fractions for which they were paid.

needlecrafts, swimming, and arts and crafts. Five schools had the services of a French assistant (e). In about a quarter of the schools, parents participated in day-to-day work and helped in such activities as cooking, games, swimming, supervision on school trips or library work.

ACCOMMODATION

15. Two-thirds of the schools had accommodation which was generally satisfactory for the range of work being undertaken, although in some cases there were minor shortcomings or a major deficiency in one specific subject area. In the remaining third of the schools, facilities for several subjects were not considered adequate.

16. Fourteen of the schools were purpose-built. Twenty-two of the schools were housed in ex-secondary accommodation and just over half of these had been adapted for middle school use. Adaptations included internal remodelling according to more open designs, the provision of facilities for home studies in former boys' schools and the conversion of specialist rooms for the teaching of other subjects, in some cases as specialist accommodation and in others as ordinary classrooms. Except for one school which occupied modified primary and secondary buildings, the remaining schools in the survey had ex-primary accommodation ; all of these had been adapted for middle school purposes. Modifications often included the provision of specialist accommodation, particularly for science, home studies and arts and crafts, and the provision of showers, changing rooms and WCs.

17. In over two-thirds of the schools, no major modifications were in progress or planned to start within two years. In the remainder, planned adaptations most often involved the provision of showers and changing rooms and the improvement of playing fields and WCs.

18. All the schools except one had a hall, and just under two-thirds had separate dining facilities. Just over half the sample had some form of temporary accommodation which varied from one or two temporary classrooms in almost a fifth of the schools to five or more temporary classrooms in six schools. Such accommodation was normally used for general class teaching, but in a few cases for other activities such as music, art, home studies, mathematics or science. Three of the schools were accommodated on split sites.

19. Forty schools had libarary accommodation, some of which had been created out of space made available as a result of falling rolls. Some schools had purpose-built libraries with large collections of books and other resources, sometimes managed by full- or part-time ancillaries. In just under a third of the sample, there were resource centres separate from library accommodation.

20. Table 24 shows the number of schools which had teaching areas specifically designated for work in particular subjects or areas of the curriculum. In general, older pupils were taught more often in these designated teaching areas than younger pupils ; differences in the extent to which children in the various year groups had access to designated teaching areas are summarised in relation to specific subjects in Chapter 7 of the report.

21. In most schools, ordinary classrooms were used for English, mathematics, history, geography and religious education and were generally adequate for the work which was undertaken. Very few schools had a drama room or studio ; some ordinary classrooms used for drama were rather small. The accommodation provided for children withdrawn for extra help with reading ranged from designated teaching areas to accommodation such as changing rooms.

22. Accommodation for the teaching of French was generally adequate ; the ordinary classrooms used provided suitable space for papers and artefacts to be displayed and film strips and slides to be shown. Just under two-thirds of the schools had accommodation which was considered satisfactory for class music teaching, and just under a third had suitable practice rooms for instrumental teaching. Storage provision for musical instruments and other equipment was satisfactory in almost half the sample. In half the schools accommodation for art provided suitable conditions and sufficient space for the activities undertaken. Deficiencies in lighting, furnishing, storage provision or power supplies were each reported in a minority of schools, more commonly where designated teaching areas were used for wood and metalcrafts as well as for art. In the majority of schools, the accommodation for craft, design and technology was adequate for the range of work, though in a number, there were deficiencies in storage, furnishings, or space. Very often, younger pupils had craft activities in classrooms which were not suitably equipped and could only be used for simple model-making using less resistant materials such as paper or card.

137

23. In a large majority of the schools, accommodation was considered generally adequate for the work being done in home studies ; the only major deficiency noted was lack of good storage provision in a considerable number of schools. About a third of the areas designated for the teaching of science were rather small, ie less than 65 sq.m., and a similar proportion lacked main services. Many science areas did not have satisfactory storage facilities.

24. In general, the schools had appropriate accommodation for gymnastics ; a third of them had a separate gymnasium in addition to a hall. In a small number of cases halls were too small or served as thoroughfares. Just over half the schools had satisfactory changing accommodation for both boys and girls. In other schools, there were difficulties over changing arrangements because facilities were too small or badly sited. One-fifth of the schools had only one changing room or were without proper facilities altogether. Three-quarters of the schools were equipped with showers but these facilities were often available to one sex only or insufficient for the numbers needing to use them. In most cases, playing fields were properly maintained, though a number were poorly drained and some had been damaged as a result of free access by the general public or by vandalism outside school hours. In about a third of the schools, hard playing areas had unsatisfactory features such as broken surfaces or excessive slopes.

RESOURCES

25. Two-thirds of the schools had resources considered to be generally adequate for the range of work being undertaken, but in many there were deficiencies in one or two specific subjects.[1] There was no evidence that, in general, the small schools had significantly poorer resources than the medium-sized or large schools.

26. The quality and quantity of course books and information books varied widely from school to school and subject to subject (Table 25). Many libraries were well stocked with information books, though frequently there were deficiencies in specific subject areas, particularly in home studies, religious education, art and design, needlecrafts, physical education, and craft, design and technology. Often there were not enough suitably challenging books for abler children or sufficient information books of good quality suitable for less able pupils. In many areas, school library services were making a valuable

[1] More detailed comments about resources for specific subjects are made in Chapter 7.

contribution to book provision, particularly in support of project work. Three-quarters of the schools had a reasonable range and quantity of fiction books. Most schools had classroom collections of fiction, sometimes supplemented by books in year bases or central libraries. Good quality fiction was often associated with the implementation of overall reading policies and with the availability of teachers with a particular interest in children's literature. In some schools not enough interesting fiction at an appropriate level of difficulty was provided either for more able or less able pupils.

27. Almost all the schools had equipment which was satisfactory in quality and quantity for the work being undertaken in modern languages and in science. About three-quarters had adequate equipment for physical education. In each of the remaining subjects, the provision of equipment was unsatisfactory in at least a quarter of the schools. (Table 26) To supplement the provision of books and equipment and to provide more appropriate work for their pupils, teachers in many of the schools prepared their own teaching materials.

28. All the schools had audio-recording equipment, at least one record player and equipment for projecting film slides, film strips and overhead transparencies. Every school but one had at least one film projector ; the same number had at least one radio and all but two had at least one television set. Over half the sample had video-recording equipment ; this was more commonly found in the large and medium-sized schools than in the small schools. Almost every school had records, tapes and maps. Three-quarters had collections of photographs and rather more had sets of slides. About three-quarters of the schools supplemented their resources by borrowing materials from museum loan services. All the schools had duplicating equipment and all but three had photocopying facilities.

29. Statistical analyses were employed to see if there were any significant associations between the adequacy of resources and the overall quality of the work in the schools. Standards in the schools with above average resources were significantly higher than in the schools with below average resources.[1] The quality and quantity of resources was also associated with the strength of the head's influence, a second factor strongly associated with standards of work.

30. The relationship between the adequacy of resources and the quality of work in specific subjects was also examined. There was a fairly strong

---

[1] For further details, see Appendix 2, Statistical notes.

association between quality and quantity of resources and the standards of work in each of the following subjects : geography, science, French, craft, design and technology, needlecrafts, music, mathematics, history, home studies, and physical education. For each of these subjects, particularly the first four, better resources were associated with higher standards of work.

31. When book resources alone were considered, better book provision was strongly associated with higher standards of work in craft, design and technology, geography, religious education, and history, and was associated fairly strongly with higher standards in science, needlecrafts, and French.[1]

ANNEX TO APPENDIX 1

Table 15 The percentage of teachers with different initial qualifications*

	BEd graduates	Other graduates	Other qualified teachers	Numbers of teaching staff
Heads	0%	17%	83%	48
Teachers (excluding heads)	12%	16%	74%	955
All teachers	11%	15%	74%	1003

* The percentages in this table have been rounded to the nearest whole number.

---

[1] For further details, see Appendix 2, Statistical notes.

Table 16 The phase-training backgrounds of teachers* holding special responsibilities

	** Heads	Deputy heads	Senior teachers	Teachers coordinating year groups	*** Teachers with special curricular responsibilities
3−8 phase	0%	0%	4%	1%	1%
5−11 phase	2%	4%	7%	6%	5%
7−11 phase	4%	11%	14%	19%	14%
Middle years phase	2%	4%	4%	8%	16%
Junior/secondary phase	44%	40%	29%	29%	25%
Secondary phase	44%	42%	43%	37%	38%
Number of teachers	48	57	28	156	584

* A teacher may appear in more than one column.
** 4% of headteachers were graduates who had not taken initial training courses.
*** 1% of teachers with special curricular responsibilities were graduates who had not taken initial training courses.

Table 17 Curricular areas and subjects related to which teachers had taken main subject in initial training

Curricular areas and subjects	Number of schools having at least one teacher who in initial training had taken a main subject related to the curricular area or the subject	Number of teachers who in initial training had taken a main subject related to the curricular area or the subject*	Number of teachers who in initial training had taken a main subject related to the curricular area or the subject, and who were teaching that subject or in that curricular area*
Humanities	48	268	215
English	47	253	212
Arts and crafts	47	193	132
Science	48	153	97
Physical education	45	138	100
Mathematics	45	130	112
Modern languages	45	96	75
Music	41	71	57
Home studies	31	40	34
Rural studies	15	19	3
Remedial education	4	4	3

*The total number of teachers in this column does not equal the total number of teachers in the survey, since some of the teachers had taken more than one main subject in their initial training.

Table 18   The constituent subjects of curricular areas taken by teachers as main subjects in their initial training

Curricular areas	Subjects	Number of schools having at least one teacher who had studied the subject as a main subject in initial training	Number of teachers who had taken the subject as a main subject in initial training*
Humanities	History	48	176
	Geography	45	156
	Religious education	34	64
	Environmental studies	15	22
	Social studies	12	16
	Humanities	4	5
English	English	47	236
	Drama	23	29
Arts and crafts	Art and design	46	135
	Craft, design and technology	26	32
	Needlecrafts	24	27
Physical education	Physical education	45	132
	Dance	6	6
Modern Languages	French	44	87
	Other modern foreign languages	15	20

*Most teachers had studied more than one main subject in their initial training. Because of this, the total number of entries related to each curricular area does not equal the total number of teachers who had studied main subjects related to each of the curricular areas, as shown in Table 17.

Table 19 Types of in-service course attended during the three years preceding the survey

Type of in-service course attended	Number of teachers attending
Single session or one-day courses (local/regional)	1046
Sessions over a number of weeks (local/regional)	1015
Course of two or three consecutive days (local/regional)	378
Course of more than three consecutive days (local/regional)	119
Short course (national)	71
One term course (national)	10
One year course (national)	27
All types of in-service courses	2666
Total number of teachers in the sample schools	1003

Table 20 The age of teachers in the sample – by size of school

| Size of school | Number of teachers in each age band | | | | |
	Under 25	25–29	30 +	Unclassified	Total
1–240	7	17	91	2	117
241–480	46	118	323	1	488
481 +	45	99	253	1	398
Total	98	234	667	4	1003

Table 21 Number of teachers by length of teaching experience – by size of school

| Size of school | Terms of teaching experience | | | | |
	0–2	3–14	15–29	30 +	Total
1–240	7	14	38	58	117
241–480	24	100	160	204	488
481 +	24	98	110	166	398
Total	55	212	308	428	1003

Table 22 The number of teachers on each scale

Scale	Size band			
	1−240	241−480	481 +	All schools
Head	9	25	14	48
Deputy head	10	30	17	57
Senior teacher	0	6	9	15
Scale 4	0	1	4	5
Scale 3	4	83	85	172
Scale 2	47	161	121	329
Scale 1*	44	177	147	368
Other	3	5	1	9
Total	117	488	398	1003

* Including probationary teachers.

Table 23 Pupil-teacher ratio by size of school*

P-t ratios	Small schools (up to 240 pupils)	Medium-sized schools (241−480 pupils)	Large schools (over 480 pupils)
Up to 14	2		
14.1−16	5		
16.1−18	1	4	1
18.1−20	1	7	1
20.1−22		10	8
22.1−24		4	3
24.1−26			1
Number of schools	9	25	14
Average PTR	15.4	20.2	21.2

* For comparison, in January 1980 the average pupil-teacher ratio for all 9−13 schools was 20.2:1.

Table 24 The number of schools which had designated teaching areas – by subject

Subject	Number of schools
Physical education	48
Science	48
Home studies	47
Art and design	45
Music	43
Craft, design and technology	42
Needlecrafts	39
Modern languages	28
Mathematics	11
Geography	10
History	9
Religious education	8
English	7

Table 25 The quality and quantity of books – by subject

Subject	Adequate quantities of books	Books of satisfactory quality	Books of satisfactory quality and quantity
Mathematics	45	43	41
Modern languages	36	41	35
English	35	39	34
History	34	38	33
Science	32	34	27
Geography	30	27	22
Music	28	33	25
Craft, design and technology	17	25	17
Home studies	17	30	17
Religious education	17	22	14
Art and design	16	25	15
Needlecrafts	12	30	12
Physical education	6	11	6

The assessments relate to the range of work being undertaken.

Table 26   The quality and quantity of equipment – by subject

Subject	Adequate quantities of equipment	Equipment of satisfactory quality	Equipment of satisfactory quality and quantity
Modern languages	43	43	42
Science	43	45	43
Physical education	42	39	37
History	39	37	37
Home studies	36	36	34
Craft, design and technology	35	36	32
Art and design	34	38	33
English	34	38	34
Mathematics	34	39	33
Geography	33	32	31
Music	31	38	29
Needlecrafts	29	34	28

The assessments relate to the range of work being undertaken.

Appendix 2   Statistical notes

1. Chapters 2 and 3 and Appendix I report associations between some characteristics of the schools and the standards of work achieved. This appendix provides more details of these associations and an outline of the statistical methodology used.

2. For each school there were fifteen dependent variables reflecting the standards of work achieved. These variables were the grades[1] for the fourteen separate subjects which are shown on Table 27, and for each school, the overall score calculated as the average of these grades.

3. In the statistical analyses, a considerable number of independent variables were used to see if they were associated with the overall standards of work achieved in the schools.[2] They included variations in pupil-teacher ratios, the length of teaching experience of staff, the age-ranges for which the teachers were trained, the number of designated teaching areas and the organisation of the curriculum in terms of separate subjects or subject combinations. None of these variables was significantly associated with the schools' overall scores.[3] Four major variables emerged as significantly associated with the schools' overall scores. One was the size of the school and another was the degree of subject teaching. The other two were the quality and quantity of resources and the strength of the head's influence.

---

[1] In each inspection HMI indicated the general standard of the children's work in each subject by awarding grades on a six-point scale ranging from 'very good' to 'very poor'.

[2] It must be borne in mind that each of the independent variables in the sample varied within a limited range and nothing can be said about the effects of these variables on standards of work in schools where they operate outside these ranges.

[3] Failure to find such associations does not necessarily mean that no associations existed. However, it is likely that any associations with the schools' scores were weaker or more subtle than those established for the four major variables.

4. In each school, for each of the fourteen subjects, assessments were made for resources on a three-point scale for quality and a four-point scale for quantity. Five types of resources were separately assessed : books, teacher-prepared materials, commercial A-V materials, equipment and apparatus, and consumable materials. The average of all these assessments was calculated for each school and was used as the independent variable for resources.

5. Each inspection team was asked to comment on the influence of the head upon the school. The strength of that influence was subsequently rated on a three-point scale : strong influence, moderate influence, and little influence.

6. In the main, the variables for the analyses were derived from either continuous data, or ordinal ratings, or classificatory data.[1] Some data, such as data related to the size of the school, were continuous. Where ordinal ratings (such as those for resources) were averaged over many values, the result was treated as a continuous variable. In the analysis the three-point rating scale for the strength of the head's influence and other ordinal data were treated both as continuous and as classificatory data[2] but no significant differences emerged from the different treatments. The overall school score, being the average of the grades awarded for a large number of subjects, was treated as continuous.

7. One way of looking at the effects of the independent variables is to see how much of the total variance in the schools' overall scores can be explained by each of the independent variables. The list below shows what percentage of the total variance was explained by each of the four major independent variables in isolation :

Resources. . .39 per cent

Strength of head's influence. . .16 per cent
Subject teaching : By first definition[3] 15 per cent
                                By second definition[3] 10 per cent

Size of school[4]. . .9 per cent

---

[1] Continuous data are measured on scales whose intervals are in some sense equal. Ordinal data are measured on scales whose points have a clear ordering, though little or nothng is known about the relative magnitude of the intervals between the points. Classificatory data are not measured on any scale and serve only to distinguish various subsets of the data.

[2] GLIM-3 the statistical package used, is similar to other multivariate packages in that it has no facilities for dealing with ordinal data as such.

[3] See Figure 1 for the first and second definitions of subject teaching.

[4] In an additional analysis, Student's 't' test was used to test for the significance of the difference in overall scores of schools with 360 or more pupils on roll, and those with fewer pupils. The difference was significant at the 5 per cent level, with the larger schools tending to have the better scores.

8. Each of these four variables was significantly associated with the schools' overall score ; significance was established by F-tests with p less than 0.05. When taken together (and using only the first definition of subject teaching) these variables accounted for 65 per cent of the total variance, a little less than the sum of the individual contributions, due to some modest correlations between the variables.

9. Of the other independent variables, most were found to explain little or none of the variance, and the remaining few, though significantly affecting the variance, were subsumed within one or other of the four major variables. An example was the strength of the deputy head's influence. That portion of the variance in the overall scores explained by the strength of the deputy's influence was also almost completely explained by the strength of the head's influence, though the converse did not hold : a large portion of the head's influence could not be explained by the strength of the deputy's influence.

10. Another way of looking at the effects of each of the variables is to compare the mean overall score of those schools which had higher than average values of an independent variable with the mean scores of those which had lower than average value. These comparisons are shown in Figure 1.

11. The other fourteen dependent variables, the grades awarded for the quality of work in each subject, were ordinal variables measured on six-point scales. At the time of the survey there were no generally accepted methods and software for multivariate analyses with ordinal dependent variables. Analyses of these fourteen variables were confined to associations with resources and with the degree of subject teaching. The measure of association chosen was Kendall's rank correlation co-efficient. The rank correlation co-efficients are shown in Table 27. Those co-efficients which were not statistically significant have been omitted, but a number of those that are shown have quite low values and should be treated with some caution.

Figure 1 *Effects of certain variables on the standards of work achieved.*

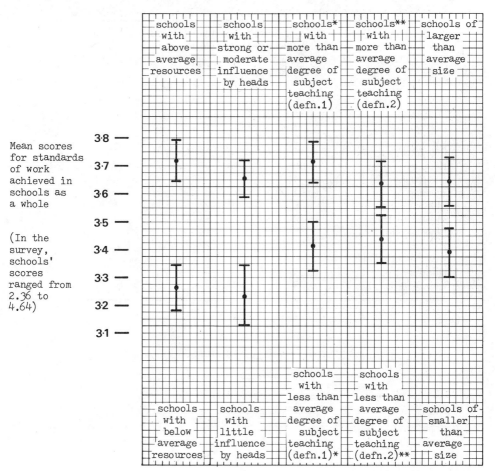

Mean scores for standards of work achieved in schools as a whole

(In the survey, schools' scores ranged from 2.36 to 4.64)

*   Definition 1: subject teaching in terms of the proportion of teachers who spent over half their week teaching one specific subject.

** Definition 2: subject teaching in terms of the proportion of teaching undertaken by teachers who had studied the subjects they taught as main subjects in initial training.

A range of one standard error around each mean score is shown. The standard errors are quite large but no conclusions were drawn from this form of analysis about the significance of a relationship between the overall scores and each of the five variables shown. F-tests based on the proportion of variance explained were used to establish significance.

The term 'resources' refers to material resources, for example books, equipment and apparatus, consumable materials.

Table 27 *Correlations between certain variables and grades awarded for specific subjects*

Subject	Rank correlation between grade awarded and :		
	Assesment of resources	Degree of subject teaching	
		1st definition	2nd definition
English	—	—	—
Art and design	.19	—	—
CDT	.48	.27	.21
Religious education	—	.22	.21
History	.35	—	—
Geography	.54	—	.24
Science	.51	—	.18
Mathematics	.35	.32	.18
Music	.36	.34	.20
Physical education	.28	.36	.32
French	.50	.27	—
Health education	—	—	—
Home studies	.34	—	—
Needlecrafts	.43	—	—

Appendix 3   Heads' questionnaires

```
                                    | School Survey Number  _____ |
DEPARTMENT OF EDUCATION AND SCIENCE | (for official use only |__|__|__||
                                    |_____ Form A1 9/13|

NATIONAL MIDDLE SCHOOL SURVEY

HEAD TEACHERS QUESTIONNAIRE

BASIC SCHOOL INFORMATION
```

1. LEA ....

2. Name of School ....

3. LEA and School number .... | / |
                                            |_____|

4. Address of School ....

   ....

   ....

5. School telephone number ....

6. Name of Headteacher ....

7. Please indicate your teaching experience in
   completed years.

	Teaching prior to Headship	Head
Primary		
Middle		
Secondary		
Other		

153

```
 _____
|                    _____      |
| Survey Number      |  |  |  |  |    |
|(For official use only) |__|__|__|   |
|                                     |
|                    Form Al 9/13     |
|_____|
```

8. Please give the number on roll.

Boys |__|____|____|

Girls |__|____|____|

TOTAL |__|____|____|

9. Please give the number on roll at end
    of last academic year.

|__|__|__|

10. Please give the estimated number likely
    to be on roll at end of next academic
    year, ie July 1981.

|__|__|__|

11. Please give the number on roll in each
    year group (ages as at 31 August 1980).

10+ |__|___|__|

11+ |__|___|__|

12+ |__|___|__|

13+ |__|___|__|

12. Please enter here the number of pupils who
    were admitted in the Autumn term in advance
    of what would have been their normal age of
    entry (9+ as at 31 August 1980.)

9+ |__|___|__|

```
 _____
| Survey Number           _____ |
| (For official use only) |  |  | ||
|                            |_|_|_||
|_____Form A1 9/13|
```

13. How many schools at the beginning of the present academic year, <u>each</u> contributed:

    i.   Less than 10% of your intake   `|___|___|`

    ii. 11-20% of your intake   `|___|___|`

   iii. 21-30% of your intake   `|___|___|`

    iv. More than 30% of your intake `|___|___|`

14. At the end of the academic year 1978/9 to how many upper or other secondary schools did you transfer:

    i.   Less than 10% of pupils at 13+

    ii. 11-20% of pupils at 13+

   iii. 21-30% of pupils at 13+

    iv. More than 30% of pupils at 13+

15. Please give the approximate percentage of pupils who live more than three miles from the school.

    `|  |  |  |`
    `|__|__|`

16. Please give an approximate percentage for the pupils in your school who belong to the following broad ethnic groups:

BRITISH /NORTH EUROPEAN/
eg family origins: UK, Irish,   `|  |  |`
Polish, Ukrainian etc   `|__|__|`

BRITISH /MEDITERRANEAN/
eg family origins: Cypriot,   `|  |  |`
Italian, Spanish etc   `|__|__|`

```
 _____
|                         _____     |
| Survey Number          |   |   |   |   | |
|(For official use only) |___|___|___|   | |
|                        Form A1 9/13    | |
|_____|
```

BRITISH /AFRO-CARIBBEAN/   _____
eg family origins Jamaican, Trinidadian, | | |
Nigerian, Ghanaian etc. |___|___|

BRITSH /ASIAN/   _____
eg Sikh, Muslim, Hindu, Chinese | | |
                                              |___|___|

BRITISH /ARAB/   _____
eg Yemeni, Somali | | |
                                              |___|___|

17. Please give a brief account of any significant social factors and their
influence on the life and work of the school. (NB such influences may be
beneficial or detrimental).

DEPARTMENT OF EDUCATION AND SCIENCE

ACCOMMODATION AND RESOURCES

ACCOMMODATION

```
┌─────────────────────────────────────────┐
│  Survey Number                           │
│  (For official use only)  ┌──┬──┬──┐     │
│                           │  │  │  │     │
│                           └──┴──┴──┘     │
│                              Form A2 9/13 │
└─────────────────────────────────────────┘
```

1. Please enter the appropriate coding to describe your school buildings

    1= Purpose built middle school,

    2= Former primary school with additions or modifications for
    middle school purposes,

    3= Former primary school without additions or modifications
    for middle school purposes,

    4= Former secondary school with additions or modifications
    for middle school purposes,

    5= Former secondary school without additions or modifications
    for middle school purposes,

    6= Other (please specify) ....

    ....

2. Please describe any additions or modifications which have been made to your
    school building and/or its site for middle school purposes.

3. Please specify any further major additions or modifications which are now in
    progress or planned to start within two years.

4. Please give the data at which the school was first designated a middle
    school.

5. Is the accommodation on a single site?

    1 = YES   2= NO   ┌──────┐
                                              │   │
                                              └──────┘

157

```
Survey Number
(For official use only) |  |  |  ||
                                    |
                              Form A2 9/13|
```

6. Please give brief details of any temporary accommodation.

7. Please indicate if accommodation includes the following

    If YES please enter 1

    If NO please enter 2

    Hall

    Dining space separate
    from hall

    Library

    Resource centre separate
    from library

8. RESOURCES

    Please indicate the location of book collections and other resources
    (More than one box may be ticked)

	Books	other resources
Central collection		
Classroom collection		
Subject collection		

9. If there is, in your school, a central book collection how is it classified?

    Dewey: please enter 1

    Not classified: please enter 2

    Other systems: please enter 3 and specify

10. If there are central collections do they have:
    If YES please enter 1. If No please enter 2.

	Books	other resources
a catalogue?		
a subject index?		

```
┌──────────────────────────────────────────┐
│ Survey Number                   ┌──┬──┬──┐ │
│ (For official use only)         │  │  │  │ │
│                                 └──┴──┴──┘ │
│                              Form A2 9/13  │
└──────────────────────────────────────────┘
```

11.   Does the school borrow from a local authority service (eg. Schools Library
                                                                    Service).

If YES please enter 1

If NO please enter 2

Books		
Fiction	Non Fiction	other resources

12.   For the supply of books do you make use of a local authority system for:

IF YES please enter 1   Purchasing

If NO please enter 2   Processing

13.   Does the school receive any professional help from a Schools Library
      Service for the purpose of:

If YES please enter 1   Library/resource
                              organisation
If NO please enter 2
                              Book selection

14.   Are there opportunities for pupils to purchase books at school from:

If YES please enter 1   Book shop?

If NO please enter 2   Book club?

                              other source?
                              (please specify)

15.   Which of the following resources are there in the school?

If YES please enter 1   Audio tapes

If NO please enter 2   Audio cassettes

                              Audio tapes

                              Video cassettes

159

15 (Continued)

```
| Survey Number                        |
| (For official use only) |  |  |  ||
|                         |__|__|__|__||
|_____Form A2 9/13 |
```

Film strips	___
Slides /sets/	___
Films	___
Film loops	___
Illustrations	___
Photographs	___
Maps	___
Records	___
Models	___

16. How many of each of these items of audio-visual and reprographic equipment are there in the school? Please give the number in each case.

Typewriter	___	Film loop projector	___
Duplicator	___	Overhead projector	___
Photocopier	___	Episcope	___
Record Player	___	Radio	___
Reel tape recorder	___	Television (Black & White)	___
Audio casssette recorder	___	Television (colour)	___
Induction loop with headphones	___	Video Recorder (Black & White)	___
Junction box& headphones	___	Video recorder (colour)	___
Play-back machine	___	Camera - still	___
Film strip/ Slide projector	___	Camera - cine	___
Film projector	___	Photographic enlarger	___

17. Did the school make use of a Museum Service during the last school year for any of the following purposes:

If YES please enter 1

If NO please enter 2

Loans of materials	___
Visits	___
Speakers	___

160

DEPARTMENT OF EDUCATION AND SCIENCE

NATIONAL MIDDLE SCHOOL SURVEY

STAFFING

NOTES FOR THE COMPLETION OF THE STAFFING FORM (A3, SHEET 1).

COLUMNS A AND B

Please enter the surnames of the staff in block capital letters followed by
initials, eg GRIMSHAW J P and number from the top of the sheet. Please indicate
title as appropriate. Start with the Head at 1, the Deputy at 2, then the rest
of the staff according to Burnham category. Please use alphabetical order
within each category.

COLUMN C SCALE OF PRESENT POST

Using the following codes, please enter the scale of the present post

    for the Head (at number 1) .... HM

    for the Deputy Head .... DH

    for the Senior Teachers .... ST

    for Salary Scales 4-1 4-1

    Probationers LI

    Other staff concerned with instruction -
    instructors, foreign language assistant .... OS

    Part-time External, eg Advisory
    teacher, peripatetic teachers .... EX

COLUMN D   INITIAL QUALIFICATIONS (INCLUDING OVERSEAS QUALIFICATIONS RECOGNISED
IN THIS COUNTRY)

    Please enter the code to indicate initial qualification.

    for BEd .... BE

    *for Graduate with post-graduate training .... TG

    *for Other Graduates .... OG

    for Other Qualified Teachers .... QT

161

for All Other Cases .... OT

*Graduate equivalent qualifications /as recognised by Burnham provisions/ should be included.

COLUMN E   Please enter the code to indicate qualifications, eg degree or college main subject(s). If there is only one main subject enter in column I if two main subjects use columns I and II etc. Where there is no subject entry please write NN.

English .... EN	French .... FR
Art and Craft .... AR	Other Modern Foreign Language ... MF
Craft Design & Technology ..... CD	Social Studies .... SS
RE .... RE	Environmental Studies .... ES
History .... HY	Rural Studies .... RS
Geography .... GY	Humanities .... HU
Science .... SC	Health Education .... HE
Mathematics .... MA	Home Studies..................... HS
Music .... MU	Library/Resources............... LR
Physical Education .... PE	Needlecraft .... NC
Dance .... DA	Remedial Teaching .... RT
Drama .... DR	

Drama .... DR

If the exact subject is not shown, a closely related subject may be entered eg 'physics' may be entered as science. If there is no closely related subject, please enter 01, 02, 03, etc., under 'other' and name each subject in the table headed COLUMN E on the reverse of the Staffing Sheet.

COLUMN F   Please enter the code to indicate initial phase training.

3 - 8 years ....(Young children)......... YC

5 - 11 years ....(Primary)................ PR

7 - 11 years ....(Junior)................ JU

Middle years .... MY

Junior/Secondary .... JS

Secondary .... SE

COLUMN G   QUALIFICATIONS SUBSEQUENT TO INITIAL QUALIFICATION

Please use the code to indicate additional qualifications.

If None .... NN

BEd .... BE

Other 1st degree .... OG

Higher Degree .... HG

Diploma* .... DA

* Qualifications that entitle the teacher to incremental credit.

COLUMN H   AGE

Please enter age in completed years.

COLUMN I   NUMBER OF COMPLETED TERMS TEACHING

Please enter the number of completed terms teaching 1,2....etc
as appropriate. If 99 <u>or more</u> please <u>enter 99.</u>

COLUMN J   TIME AT PRESENT SCHOOL IN COMPLETED TERMS (NB.   'Present School' is
                                                            intended to indicate
                                                            the existing school
                                                            since designated
                                                            'middle')

Please enter the numbers of completed terms as 1,2 ... etc as
appropriate.

COLUMN K   FULL-TIME AND PART-TIME SERVICE

Please enter code 10 for each teacher in full-time service. For
teachers serving part-time enter full-time equivalent to the nearest
half day, eg 3½ days would appear as 07.

COLUMN L   SPECIAL CURRICULAR RESPONSIBILITY

      Please indicate by entering the following code if the teacher has special curricular responsibility. Should the teacher have more than two curricular responsibilities enter the two important ones. If the teacher has no special curricular responsibilities please put zeros (00) in both boxes.

Responsible for:

English .... EN	French .... FR
Art and Craft .... AR	Other Foreign Language .... MF
Craft Design & Technology........ CD	Social Studies .... SS
RE .... RE	Environmental Studies .... ES
History .... HY	Rural Studies .... RS
Geography .... GY	Humanities .... HU
Science .... SC	Health Education .... HE
Mathematics .... MA	Home Studies .... HS
Music .... MU	Library/Resources .... LR
Physical Education .... PE	Needlecraft .... NC
Dance .... DA	Remedial Teaching .... RT
Drama .... DR	English as a Second Language E2

                              Other, please enter OA, OB, OC, etc for each responsibility in the table marked COL.L on the reverse side of the staffing form.

COLUMN M   SPECIAL ORGANISATIONAL RESPONSIBILITY

      Please indicate by entering the following code if the teacher has special organisational responsibility. Should the teacher have more than two organisational responsibilities enter the two most important ones. If the teacher has no special organisational responsibilities please put zeros (00) in both boxes.

      Deputy Head .... DH

      Year group co-ordinator .... YG

      Team leader or co-ordinator .... TL

Liaison with first schools .... LF

Liaison with upper schools .... LU

Special unit .... SU

Home-school liaison .... HL

Other .... OT

COLUMN N   AGE GROUPS

The age groups are listed according to age of pupils at
31 August next.

COLUMN O

For this column please calculate the percentage of time in the week
for which the teacher teaches that subject to each year group.
Please give percentages to the nearest whole number. Please do <u>not</u>
make subject double entries. In particular remedial work should be
entered under remedial and not under the subjects involved.
Percentages of time for subject combinations under titles not shown
in COLUMN O should be entered under OTHER and the titles specified in
the table on the reverse side of FORM A3 SHEET 1.

a.   Where a group extends across two years divide the time
     given by two and enter for each year.

b.   Where a group extends across three years divide by three
     and enter for each year.

c.   Where a group extends across four years divide by four
     and enter for each year.

The total percentage of time for each full-time teacher should be
100. For part-time teachers the total will be less than 100 in
accord with the entry in column K.

(The percentage of the work is calculated as follows:

$$\text{Percentage} = \frac{\text{Time given to subject}}{\text{Time given to whole curriculum}} \times 100\%$$

'Time' can be expressed in any manner eg. periods, minutes,
hours and minutes).

FORM A3 SHEET 1:9/13   Survey Number | | | |

COLUMN E SUBJECT QUALIFICATIONS KEY TO 'OTHER' SUBJECTS	
CODE	SUBJECT
01	

COLUMN L SPECIAL CURRICULAR RESPONSIBILITY KEY TO 'OTHER' RESPONSIBILITIES	
CODE	SUBJECT
0A	

FORM A3 SHEET 1:9/13   Survey Number |__|__|__|

A	B	C	D	E			F	G	H	I	J	K	L		M	
TEACHER Nº	NAME OF TEACHER	SCALE OF PRESENT POST	INITIAL QUALIFICATION	SUBJECT QUALIFICATION			PHASE TRAINING	POST EXPERIENCE QUALIFICATION	AGE	NUMBER OF COMPLETED TERMS TEACHING	TIME AT PRESENT SCHOOL IN COMPLETED TERMS	FULL-TIME EQUIVALENT	SPECIAL CURRICULAR RESPONSIBILITIES		SPECIAL ORGANISATIONAL RESPONSIBILITIES	
				I	II	III							I	II	I	II
	|MR/MRS/MISS|														
	|MR/MRS/MISS|														
	|MR/MRS/MISS|														
	|MR/MRS/MISS|														
	|MR/MRS/MISS|														
	|MR/MRS/MISS|														

FORM SHEET 1: 9/13   Survey Number |___|___|___|

N	O CURRICULUM																										
AGE GROUP	ENGLISH	ART AND CRAFT	CDT	RE	HISTORY	GEOGRAPHY	SCIENCE	MATHEMATICS	MUSIC	PHYSICAL EDUCATION	DANCE	DRAMA	FRENCH	OTHER MODERN LANGUAGE	SOCIAL STUDIES	ENVIRONMENTAL STUDIES	RURAL STUDIES	HUMANITIES	HEALTH EDUCATION	HOME STUDIES	LIBRARY	NEEDLECRAFTS	REMEDIAL	OTHER (SPECIFY OVERLEAF)	TOTAL	NON-TEACHING
10+																										
11+																										
12+																										
13+																										
10+																										
11+																										
12+																										
13+																										
10+																										
11+																										
12+																										
13+																										
10+																										
11+																										
12+																										
13+																										
10+																										
11+																										
12+																										
13+																										
10+																										
11+																										
12+																										
13+																										

Survey Number | | | | | FORM A3 SHEET 1: 9/13
               |__|__|__|__|

COLUMN 0 (continued)

Please enter here 'other' subjects taught.

Teacher Number	Subject

DEPARTMENT OF EDUCATION AND SCIENCE

RECORDS AND LIAISON

```
| Survey Number                        |
| (For official use only |  |  |  |    |
|                          Form A4 9/13|
```

1. Please indicate whether any of the following forms of records are used to facilitate transfer of children between a) First Schools and your School, b) classes within your school, c) your School and Upper School.

   IF YES enter 1
   If NO enter 2

   a.   b.   c.

   LEA Record Card

   School's own record

   Samples of work of individual pupils

   Results of standardised tests

   Class or year lists of attainment

   Other records, please specify

2. Please ring all codes for which pupil records are passed on to the upper school. (These are codings as used in Notes For Completion of the Staffing Form, Reference Column E, with the addition of E2 (English as a second language) and OT (other).)

   EN   AR   CD   RE   HY   GY   SC   MA   MU   PE   DA

   DR   FR   MF   SS   ES   RS   HU   HE   HS   NC   RT   E2   OT

   If OT is ringed please specify.
   If no subject records are passed on to the upper school, please tick. |___|

3. Were any of the following procedures used in the year 1978/9 to facilitate the transfer of pupils a) between the first school and your school, b) your school and the upper school?

   If with all schools - please enter 1
   If with some schools - please enter 2
   If with no schools - please enter 3

   Pupils making introductory visit(s)

   Staff exchange for teaching commitment

   Joint meetings of staff for curricular discussions.

   a.   b.

```
 _____
|                      _____      |
|  Survey Number      |   |   |   |     |
| (For official use only|   |   |   |    |
|                   ‾‾‾‾‾‾‾‾‾‾‾          |
|              Form A4 9/13              |
|_____|
```

3. (Continued)   a.   b.

    Feedback of comment on children's subsequent progress

    Please give a brief account of other liaison procedures.

4. Was there consultation in the year 1978/9 about the following curricular
    areas between:

    i.   Teachers in your school and those in first schools?

    ii.   Teachers in your middle school and other local middle schools?

    iii. Teachers in your school and those in the upper schools?

                If with all schools .... Please enter 1
                If with some schools........ Please enter 2
                If with no schools .... Please enter 3
                If the subject is not taught in your school....... Please enter 9

	i.	ii.	iii.
English			
Art			
Craft, Design & Technology			
Religious Education			
History			
Geography			
Science			
Mathematics			
Music			
Physical Education			
French			
Other Modern Foreign Languages			
English as a Second Language			
Social Studies			

4. (Continued)

Environmental Studies

Rural Studies

Humanities

Remedial Work

Health Education

Home Studies

Needlecrafts

Multi-racial Education

Other (please specify)

5. Is there a system in use for the assessment of literacy(a) laid down by the school, (b) laid down by the LEA?

If YES please enter 1   School system
If NO please enter 2

If YES in either case please give details   LEA system

6. Is there a language/literacy testing policy specifically for pupils for whom English is a second language (a) laid down by the school (b) laid down by the LEA?

If YES please enter 1   School
If NO please enter 2

                                               LEA

7. Is there a system in use for the assessment of numeracy(a) laid down by the school (b) laid down by the LEA?

If YES please enter 1
If NO please enter 2   School

                                              LEA system

172

```
 _____
| Survey                         |
|(For official use only  |__|__|__| |
|                  Form A4   9/13|
|_____|
```

8. Please indicate the frequency with which each age group is given some form
    of standardised test.

    If not at all please enter 1
    If once a year please enter 2
    If twice a year please enter 3
    If more than twice a year please enter 4.

	Language				Mathematics			
	10+	11+	12+	13+	10+	11+	12+	13+
More able pupils								
Average pupils								
Less able pupils								

Please specify the standardised tests used and indicate the age and ability
range to which they are applied.

DEPARTMENT OF EDUCATION AND SCIENCE

Survey Number
(For official use only | | | | |

Form A5 9/13

ORGANISATION

1. Is there a written job specification for the deputy headteacher?

    If YES please enter 1
    If No please enter 2 | | |

2. Is there a written job specification for Year Group Leaders?

	10+	11+	12+	13+

    If YES please enter 1
    If NO please enter 2
    If NO YEAR LEADERS please enter 9

3. Is there a written job specification for teachers with curricular
    responsibilities? If so, please ring the codes for the subjects concerned.

    EN   AR   CD   RE   HY   GY   SC   MA   MU   PE   DA

    DR   FR   MF   SS   ES   RS   HU   HE   HS   NC   RT   E2

(These are codings as used in Notes for Completion of the Staffing Form,
reference Column E.)

4. Please indicate which of the following most nearly describes the
    organisation in each year.

5. Most subjects are taught by subject specialists ....Please enter 1

    Most subjects are taught by the class teacher .... Please enter 2

    There is approximately equal involvement of class teachers and subject
    specialists ......Please enter 3

10+	11+	12+	13+

174

Survey Number
(For official use only)

5. Are some subjects or activities taught in a rotational pattern?

If YES please enter 1
If NO please enter 2

IF YES:

In column A please give the title, if any, given to the rotational combination.

In column B please give the percentage of time in the week allocated to the combination.

In column C please give the span of the whole rotation in weeks.

In column D please list the subjects included, indicating the percentage of time allocated to each subject within the whole span of the rotation. These percentages should add up to 100% within each combination thus:

Music (50%), Art (25%), Dance (25%)

	A	B	C	D
10+				
11+				
12+				
13+				

9–13 Middle Schools

Survey Number
(For official use only

Form A5 9/13

6. Are there, in your school, subjects combined together?
    If so please give the titles and the subjects so brought together.
    Please tick the years involved in each case.

Title of Combined Subjects	Subject included	Years involved			
		10+	11+	12+	13+

176

Form A5 9/13

7. Using the list of subjects provided for columns O in the staffing table
    (Form A3), or any titles of combined subjects which you have used for
    question 8, please name in column A the subjects for which there are
    detailed schemes of work or general guidelines. "General guidelines" is
    intended to indicate a broad outline of what is to be taught, not going
    beyond a list of contents.

    Please make entries in one or both of columns B and C to indicate the
    originator(s) of the document(s). Choose one or more of the codes from
    the following list:

    Headteacher......... 1   If, for example there were only general
    HoD/Consultant 2   guidelines for a subject drawn up by a
    Year leader 3   Head of Department in consultation with
    Other teachers 4   an LEA adviser, an entry of 2,5, in
    LEA adviser 5   column C only would be appropriate.

    Please place a tick in column D alongside each subject if all staff
    teaching the subject have copies of the schemes or guidelines.

A	B	C	D
Subject	Detailed Scheme	General Guide Lines	Copies

Survey Number

8. For each year please state below how the teaching groups are arranged.

    (eg. Are they?

    Streamed - Classes ranked according to ability.

    Banded - Parallel classes are grouped and the groups arranged in rank
             order according to ability.

    Mixed Ability - Each class contains a full range of the ability
                    within the year group.

    NB. In your school a given year group may not fall entirely within
         any one category).

    10+

    11+

    12+

    13+

Survey Number
(For official use only)

Form A5   9/13

9. For the following are the pupils grouped into sets according to ability in the subject? If YES please enter 1   If NO please enter 2

Please ignore withdrawal groups which are dealt with in Question 12 and in Paper A6.

SUBJECT	AGE GROUPS			
	10+	11+	12+	13+
English				
Art and Craft				
Craft, Design/Technology				
RE				
History				
Geography				
Science				
Mathematics				
Music				
Physical Education				
French				
Other Modern Language				
Social Studies				
Environmental Studies				
Rural Studies				
Humanities				
Health Education				
Home Studies				
Needlecrafts				
Other (please specify)				

Survey Number
(For official use only) |__|__|__|__|

Form A5 9/13

10. Please indicate whether you use any of the following kinds of organisation for the teaching of exceptionally able children.

    If YES please enter 1

    If NO   please enter 2

    Withdrawal of individuals

    Withdrawal of groups

    Long term withdrawal to a
    special class

    Supernumerary teacher
    working with a class

    Cooperative ways of working
    to allow regrouping of two
    or more classes

    Other (please specify)......
    ....

11. Please list in column A any registration groups which contain children of more than one academic year group. In column B please indicate the age range of each such class by entering the code for the statement which most nearly represents the current situation.

    If the majority of children are of one academic year but there are a few children of a different year group (or groups). Please enter 1

    If the children are from two academic year groups with significant numbers from each of the two years (and possibly a few children from another group (or groups). Please enter 2.

    If the children are from three or more academic year groups with significant numbers in at least three years. Please enter 3.

A Class	B

Survey Number
(For official use only)

| | | |

Form   A5   9/13

12. Is the fact that you have registration groups of more than one academic year group in your school a direct result of the small total number on the school roll?

If YES please enter 1

If NO please enter 2

If NOT APPLICABLE enter 9

Survey Number
(For official use only)

Form A5   9/13

13. For the purposes of this analysis please give, to the nearest whole number,
the percentage of the week allocated to each subject.

ANALYSIS OF TIMETABLE				
	AGE GROUPS			
SUBJECT	10+	11+	12+	13+
ENGLISH				
ART				
RE				
HISTORY				
GEOGRAPHY				
SCIENCE				
MATHEMATICS				
MUSIC				
PE				
DANCE				
DRAMA				
FRENCH				
CRAFT, DESIGN and TECHNOLOGY				
OTHER MODERN FOREIGN LANGUAGE				
SOCIAL STUDIES				
ENVIRONMENTAL STUDIES				
RURAL STUDIES				
HUMANITIES				
HEALTH EDUCATION				
HOME STUDIES				
NEEDLECRAFTS				
OTHER*				
TOTALS	100	100	100	100

* Please specify

182

Appendix 4　Summaries of HMI schedules

During the survey, HMI made their assessments in accordance with agreed schedules which listed a wide range of activities likely to be found in middle schools. While it was not expected that every school would necessarily include all the activities related to the items listed in the schedules, it was thought likely that each school would cover most of these, though the precise selection of activities would be dependent on the individual circumstances of each school. The schedules covered the following aspects of the work of the schools :

a. the organisation and management of the school, and the provision made for children's social and personal education

b. language and literacy

c. mathematics

d. science

e. modern languages

f. art and design

g. craft, design and technology

h. music

i. history

j. geography

k. religious education

l. home studies and needlecrafts

m. physical education

n. health education

o. provision for children with special educational needs.

ITEMS COMMON TO ALL SCHEDULES

For all the aspects of work listed above except a. each schedule asked HMI to report on the context of the work observed, in terms of :

   i. the nature of the accommodation

   ii. the range and quality of resources and the use made of these resources during the period of the visit

   iii. the extent to which out-of-school resources are used

   iv. the responsibilities and qualifications of the teacher or teachers with designated responsibility for the subject

   v. the criteria used for the organisation of teaching groups

   vi. the extent to which the subject is taught separately or in combination

   vii. the adequacy of the time allocation

   viii. the use made by the school of the local education authority advisory service

   ix. the schemes of work : availability, contents, extent to which they are followed, and procedures for reappraisal

   x. the methods of assessment and quality of records kept on children's achievements

   xi. the nature, extent and effectiveness of liaison between :
      a. the middle school and the first schools from which pupils are received
      b. the middle school and other middle schools in the area
      c. the middle school and the upper schools to which pupils transfer.

In addition, at the end of each schedule, HMI was asked to comment on :
      i. the general effects of having the age-range 9—13 in one school
      ii. the general effects of the size of school
      iii. the appropriateness of the work for a. children of above average ability, b. children of average ability, and c. children of below average ability.

ITEMS SPECIFIC TO PARTICULAR SCHEDULES

The following sub-sections summarise the factors referred to in schedules related to *specific* aspects of the work of the schools.

General features of the school : its organisation and management, and the provision made for children's social and personal education

1. The range and quality of opportunities provided for pupils to exercise initiative, responsibility, leadership and participation ; the response of pupils to such opportunities.

2. The characteristics of the school's catchment area.

3. Evidence of the practice and quality of pastoral care.

4. The quality of relationships between adults and pupils, and evidence on the general behaviour of pupils.

5. Evidence of arrangements made for consultation between parents and staff ; evidence of parents' involvement in the day-to-day work of the school.

6. Evidence of links with the local community.

7. The factors which influence the range of subjects taught.

8. The nature of the responsibilities carried by the head and senior staff, and the factors influencing the discharge of these responsibilities.

9. Evidence of the influence of head and senior staff on the work of the children.

10. The effects of local education authority policies on the school ; the use made by the school of the local education authority advisory service.

11. The extent to which the school succeeds in creating an environment likely to encourage learning.

12. The nature of the 'out-of-school' activities organised for the children.

Language and literacy

1. Background features over which the school has little control but which influence the 'language life' of the school.

2. Evidence on the leadership or guidance given to teachers about language.

3. The range and quality of opportunities provided for talking and listening.

4. Evidence on the attention given to drama.

5. Evidence on the provision of fiction, information and poetry books.

6. The quality of library provision.

7. The quality of children's attainment in reading ; evidence on the teaching of reading including strategies to develop and extend children's reading skills ; opportunities provided for children to read for pleasure.

8. Evidence on children's use of information and text books.

9. Opportunities provided for children to hear, read or write poetry.

10. The extent to which fiction and poetry are used in different areas of the curriculum.

11. The emphasis given to writing, the assistance given to children, and the quality of their response.

12. Evidence on each of the following aspects of the work : the teaching of handwriting, the teaching of spelling and punctuation, children's use of the current conventions of spelling and punctuation, and the standard of presentation of children's work.

13. The extent to which provision is made for slow learners and/or very able pupils.

14. Evidence of the school's awareness of out-of-school influences on children's language eg television.

Mathematics

1. The degree of attention given to the application of mathematics across the curriculum.

2. Evidence on the general style of teaching in the school, and the factors leading to the successful teaching of mathematics.

3. The extent to which opportunities are provided for children to do each of the following ; to use commonsense methods, to practise mental mathematics, to participate in oral work, to exercise choice, and to organise their own work and materials.

4. The extent to which practical activities are provided.

5. The extent to which the pupils are given opportunities to work on each of the following topics : the four operations with whole numbers, fractions and decimals ; estimation and approximation, experience with a variety of

186

measuring instruments, applications of computation, geometrical aspects of natural and man-made forms, graphical representation of data, creative work (investigations, puzzles etc.), and exploration of patterns leading to generalisations.

6. The range of topics included in courses and the proportion of children to whom the topics are taught.

7. Evidence of pupils' attitudes towards mathematics.

8. The quality of mathematical display.

9. Evidence of the use made of text books, workcards/worksheets, and broadcasts.

10. Evidence of the use of calculators and computers.

11. Extent to which the school makes provision for very able pupils, for the least able pupils, or for children whose mother tongue is not English.

12. Evidence of the extent to which local education authority guidelines influence the teaching of mathematics.

13. Evidence of liaison with parents about the mathematics course and the progress of individual children.

14. Evidence of the use made of homework.

Science

1. The extent to which the following activities are used ; pupils' practical work, teacher demonstration, discussion, reading from text books and reference books, activities from work cards, formal recording, and free writing about science.

2. Evidence of the links made between science and other subjects, particularly mathematics.

3. The extent to which opportunities are provided for children to initiate and pursue their own investigations.

4. Evidence of the suitability of content.

5. The quality of provision made for, and of development achieved in, the following activities : observation, selection of evidence or data, pattern-seeking, experimentation, explanation, application, communication, perseverance, and the safe and confident use of equipment.

6. Evidence of children's attitudes towards science.

Modern languages

1. The degree of emphasis given to each of the following four language skills : aural, reading, speaking, and writing.

2. Evidence of progression in children's aural comprehension and of the techniques used to develop this, egs listening or guessing games, performing actions in response to commands, listening to tapes.

3. Evidence of the suitability of reading tasks given to children and of the techniques used to foster reading comprehension, egs use of written materials on display, detailed study of a reader, rapid reading of a reader by the whole class, and individual reading for gist.

4. Evidence of children's progress towards independence in talking and of the techniques used to foster talk, egs choral repetition, answering questions, asking questions, group games, role-playing and dialogue, use of drama.

5. Evidence of progression in the kinds of writing done by children and of the techniques used to foster this activity egs bilingual vocabulary notebooks, copying of dialogues and stories, writing from memory, and guided composition.

6. The extent to which French is used in the classrooms.

7. The part played by background studies in the teaching of French.

Art and design

1. Evidence of the extent to which pupils are required to observe carefully and to record their observations in visual form.

2. The range of processes in art which children experience.

3. The extent to which children develop a. sensitivity to the formal elements of art, b. the ability to discriminate and make judgements, and c. the ability to evaluate their own work and that of others.

4. Evidence of opportunities provided for a. personal interpretation, and b. work within the constraints of design problems.

5. The quality of teaching methods, programmes of work, materials, tools and equipment.

6. The quality of attention given to the environment, eg displays.

7. The quality of pupils' response as evidenced by their work, language, skills, judgements and attitudes.

Craft, design and technology

1. The range of processes experienced by pupils, and the extent to which pupils are able to select the appropriate processes for the task in hand.

2. Evidence that children are required to design and make forms or structures in response to problems where the answers are not prescribed.

3. Evidence that pupils have opportunities to extend their competence in the use of graphics.

4. Evidence that children are encouraged to evaluate their own work and that of others.

5. The quality of provision for craft, design and technology eg the suitability of resources, the type of working spaces provided and the way in which they are organised, and the form of the programmes of work provided.

6. The quality of pupils' response, as illustrated by the way in which they approach the work, their ability to make judgements and their use of skills in draughtsmanship and craftsmanship.

7. The degree of attention given to the safe handling of tools and materials and to the development of safety awareness.

8. The extent of links between craft, design and technology and other areas of the curriculum.

Music

1. Evidence on the extent of instrumental teaching, the main instruments taught and the teaching arrangements employed.

2. Evidence on the contribution made by peripatetic teachers to the teaching of music.

3. The extent to which children engage in the following activities : singing ; recorder playing as a classroom activity for all ; guitar playing as a classroom

activity for all ; class music-making using instruments ; pupil-devised music-making eg original composition, improvisation ; listening ; music reading ; electronic music-making ; individual interests ; and, instrumental playing in assembly.

4. Evidence of the extent to which children develop a critical appreciation of music.

5. Evidence of the range and appropriateness of the songs taught.

6. The extent to which children are acquiring the necessary technical skills to participate in music-making by means of a. voice, and b. instruments (within the classroom).

7. The extent to which special provision is made for gifted children or less able children.

History

1. The extent to which children are helped to develop the following : an understanding of time sequence and chronology, an understanding of change and continuity, an understanding of causality and historical explanation, an ability to appreciate the points of view and circumstances of other people, an awareness of the need for evidence, an ability to use and evaluate primary and secondary historical sources, and an ability to use and evaluate historical fiction.

2. Evidence that children are given opportunities to develop the following abilities : to find information, to collate information from more than one source, to analyse and select what is useful and relevant, and to present material coherently and in an appropriate form.

3. The extent to which the work contains material from the following categories :

    i. local history

    ii. national history

    iii. world history

    iv. pre–500 AD

    v. 500–1500 AD

    vi. 1850–present.

4. The emphasis given in the work to people's lives, work and beliefs.

5. The quality of children's response in the following aspects of the work :

   a. oral work and discussion

   b. written work

   c. drama

   d. pictorial work

   e. three-dimensional work

   f. audio-visual presentation, and

   g. games and/or simulations.

Geography

1. Evidence that children have studied :

   a. what places are like

   b. how people have used and adapted their surroundings for various activities

   c. the location of places, features and activities

   d. the distribution of places, features and activities

   e. the movements of people and goods between places

   f. changes in the character of places and in the location of activities

   g. environmental or social issues relating to particular places.

2. Evidence that children have attempted to find explanations or establish relationships in connection with the topics outlined in 1.

3. Evidence that pupils have opportunities to do each of the following : use a globe ; use atlases as sources of information ; draw maps and use maps to record information ; interpret symbols, settlement features and relief from large-scale maps ; and measure distances from maps.

4. Evidence that attention has been given to each of the following topics :

    a. farming

    b. settlement

    c. industry

    d. transport

    e. landforms

    f. resources.

5. Evidence that attention has been given to each of the following areas :

    a. the locality

    b. United Kingdom

    c. Western World

    d. Communist World

    e. Developing World.

6. Evidence on the contents and types of activities used in the study of geographical topics at the time of the inspection.

7. The nature and quality of pupils' response to work requiring them to :

    a. observe

    b. collect and record information

    c. select relevant evidence

    d. present information appropriately, and

    e. recall and apply knowledge in new situations.

8. The extent to which children are given opportunities for :

    a. independent work

    b. work in groups

    c. initiative

    d. responsibility for planning work, and

    e. perseverance.

Religious education

1. The degree of emphasis given to :

   a. The Old Testament

   b. The New Testament, and

   c. The nature of the Bible and its background.

2. The attention given to world religions.

3. Evidence on the extent to which religious education is put in a broad perspective : for example, the historical development of the Church, the meaning of faith for Christians and followers of other religions, Christian and other ways of worship.

4. Evidence on the organisation, contents and effects of assemblies.

5. Evidence of the ways in which children communicate their response to religious ideas in class and assembly.

6. Evidence that children are beginning to consider major religious questions.

7. Evidence that children are being taught about the language of myth, symbolism, worship and ritual.

8. Evidence of the ways in which religious education in particular and the school in general promote the understanding of religious ideas and the formation of attitudes such as sympathy and tolerance.

Home studies and needlecrafts

1. The extent to which children are given opportunities to learn to : solve problems ; make decisions ; cooperate with others ; take responsibility ; identify priorities ; extract information ; use initiative ; work independently ; plan and complete a piece of work ; and use materials economically.

2. Evidence on the opportunities provided to extend pupils' competence in : language ; mathematical understanding ; scientific understanding ; aesthetic and sensory awareness ; manipulative skills ; and social skills.

3. Evidence that children have developed their abilities to : manage money ; manage time ; care for their clothes or personal possessions ; feed themselves sensibly ; understand rules for health ; show concern for others ; and, look after a home.

4. Evidence on the appearance of teaching areas and the use made of display.

5. Evidence on the attention given to hygiene and to teaching pupils how to handle tools and equipment appropriately and safely.

6. Evidence of links between home studies and needlecrafts and other areas of the curriculum.

Physical education

1. The extent to which opportunities are taken to develop athletics, countryside activities, dance, games, gymnastics and swimming.

2. The extent to which emphasis is placed on competition.

3. Evidence of links with work in other areas of the curriculum.

4. Evidence that children are given opportunities to do the following : observe carefully, extract information, make decisions, solve problems, identify priorities, cooperate with others, take responsibility, work independently, use initiative, transfer knowledge and skills, respond to agreed rules, show concern for personal health and hygiene, and show enjoyment in physical education.

5. Evidence that children have developed the following : movement confidence and sensitivity, manipulative skills, the ability to anticipate the

movement of people and things, use of movement to communicate feelings and ideas, the ability to cooperate and compete sensibly, a sense of purpose in movement, development of aesthetic awareness, and appropriate movement response to a variety of stimuli.

6. The extent to which children handle apparatus safely and move in a controlled manner, showing consideration for others.

7. The attention given to hygiene and appropriate dress.

8. The nature of the activities organised by teachers outside normal school hours.

Health education

1. Evidence of attention given to the following topics :

    a. the function of the human body

    b. physical and emotional changes at puberty

    c. hygiene

    d. safety

    e. environmental hazards

    f. social hazards, and

    g. interpersonal relationships.

2. Evidence that the school uses teaching materials from curriculum development projects.

3. The extent to which radio and television programmes are used regularly for health education.

4. Evidence that the school has discussed health education with a. parents, b. officers of the Area Health Authority.

Provision for children with special educational needs

In relation to each of the following groups of children :

    a. those with emotional and behavioural difficulties

    b. those having learning difficulties

    c. those having moderate learning difficulties

    d. those with impaired hearing

    e. those with physical handicaps.

1. Evidence of the patterns of teaching employed eg the balance between class work and work in withdrawal groups.

2. The adequacy of the time allocated to specialist teaching.

3. Evidence of the screening procedures used.

4. Evidence of the use of standardised tests and other procedures for the diagnosis of children's special difficulties.

5. Evidence within schemes of work for curricular subjects of references to children with special educational needs.

6. Evidence of efforts made by the school to help parents understand their children's special educational needs.

7. Evidence of the extent to which the needs of the children are being met.

Index

Major references are set in bold type.

201

V

visits (journeys) : 3.7, 4.3, 4.11, 7.9,
    7.20, 7.36, 7.55, 7.68, 7.69,
    7.117, 7.130, 7.139, 7.159, 7.161,
    7.171, 7.174, 7.188, 7.192, 7.194
  to middle schools : 6.17
  to upper schools : 6.21
voluntary activities : 2.5, 2.16, 3.8,
    4.3, 4.7, 7.9, 7.18, 7.74, 7.132,
    7.134,
work
  inspection of : 1.7
  levels of difficulty of : **2.15**, 2.31,
    5.3, 7.2, 7.12, 7.26, 7.46, 7.61,
    7.84, 7.99, 7.118, 7.120, 7.131,
    7.136, 7.145, 7.166, 7.168, 7.196,

    8.2, 8.8, **8.10**, 8.21
  standards of : 2.2, 2.8, 2.23, 2.24,
    2.30, **2.31**, **2.32**, 3.29, 7.2, 7.26,
    7.46, 7.61, 7.84, 7.99, 7.118,
    7.131, 7.134, 7.137, 7.145, 7.166,
    7.168, 7.196, 8.7, 8.11, 8.12,
    8.21, 8.22, Appendix 2
writing : 2.9, 3.23, 5.3, 7.3, 7.7, 7.8,
    7.10, **7.19—7.24**, 7.52, 7.127,
    7.164, 7.191, 7.192, 8.8

Y

year group coordinators : 2.26, 3.7,
    6.17, 6.21, 7.182, 7.185, 8.14,
    8.18

Printed in the UK for HMSO
PS 3251422 Dd.737401 C150 12/83